TIMOTÉ

OSCAR VALENCIA

BALBOA.PRESS

A DIVISION OF HAY HOUSE

Balboa Press books may be ordered through booksellers or by contacting:

Balboa Press
A Division of Hay House
1663 Liberty Drive
Bloomington, IN 47403
www.balboapress.com
844-682-1282

Interior Image Credit: Rafael Calzada

Print information available on the last page.

ISBN: 979-8-7652-4250-6 (sc)
ISBN: 979-8-7652-4251-3 (hc)
ISBN: 979-8-7652-4252-0 (e)

Library of Congress Control Number: 2023910212

Balboa Press rev. date: 05/22/2023

To my beloved wife, Martita

To my dearest children, Liz and Phool

To my great indigenous friend, the humble and
wise teacher Cuatiendioy, who taught me a different
way of seeing life, in the Amazon jungle

To my elder brothers Nelson and Héctor,
whose quest for spiritual growth led me and
inspired me to share this experience

To my younger brothers, who
suffered during my absence,

And to life, for giving me parents who taught
me how to fly, ever since I was a child.

To all of them: Thank you
Timoté

CONTENTS

FOREWORD BY THE EDITOR

The first time I saw Timoté was during a seven day seshin in Cuernavaca, Mexico. Although we did not talk, I remember him sitting in silence facing the wall. There was something different about this man.

Years later, during my seven year training at the Rochester Zen Center in upstate New York, Timoté came to participate in one of the seshins that are offered regularly at the Zen Center. I quickly recognized him and asked him why he was attracted to the Zen tradition. People from all over the world came to the Zen Center, and it was always fascinating to me to learn how they became interested in Zen.

He told me that during a business trip to Japan, he has visited a Zen Temple in the city of Sakura. The most remarkable quality of that Zen Center was the quietness and silence of the atmosphere. He told me that the only place he had experienced that silence was in the Amazon rainforest while he was an apprentice with his teacher: Cuatiendoy.

This was my first introduction to the amazing teachings of Cuatiendoy, a wise shaman living in the Amazon rainforest who possessed remarkable abilities including telepathy, a deep understanding of the subconscious, healing with herbs and orchids, communicating with animals, and overall, had a profound connection with the Earth mother of the Amazon. Timoté recorded his experiences with Cuatiendoy in a manuscript and gave me a copy. The book that you hold in your hands describes the experiences that Timoté had with Cuatiendoy, including profound metaphysical teachings that were transmitted to him.

The first thing that struck me was that Cuatiendoy did not sleep at night. Instead, he used to meditate on tree branches in full-lotus posture the whole night, which reminded me of two of the greatest Zen masters who were known for not lying down to sleep but meditated until dawn. Cuatiendoy was also a master of breathing techniques, which allowed him to change the temperature of his body and more importantly, to quiet his mind. He developed his own pranayama practices that allowed him to awaken profound psychic abilities.

Part of my research and training has been in Taoist alchemy, and what amazed me were the similarities between the teachings of Cuatiendoy and the Taoist masters, both of which are rooted in the quantum field. We can say that Cuatiendoy was immersed in the quantum field unceasingly. We can also consider Cuatiendoy a modern Druid mystic with a deep understanding of the subtle laws of the universe, herbs, and how natural cycles influence human beings.

The most important message of this book is the importance of respecting nature, and how humans have created their self-inflicted pain by not following the immutable laws of the universe, instead going against them. Cuatiendoy exposes the severe problems caused to the Amazon rainforest by the "civilized man." He shows how it is being destroyed by greed and ignorance. For context, the Amazon rainforest lost an area comparable to the size of Israel in 2020.Throughout history, great human beings have emphasized the importance of Nature in the evolution of human consciousness.

Walter Russell, who was considered the Leonardo DaVinci of the 20th Century, explained the following in his biography called "The Man Who Tapped the Secrets of the Universe": "You may command Nature to the extent only to which you are willing to obey her. You cannot intelligently obey that which you do not comprehend. Therefore I also say, ask of Nature that you may be one with her, and she will whisper her secrets to you to the extent to which you are prepared to listen".

Ralph Waldo Emerson described Nature as the embodiment of Divine Law, which is exemplified by the teachings Cuatiendoy revealed to Timoté, and can be summarized as follows: "Nature will reveal to you great teachings, but only to the extent that you approach her with humbleness, gratitude, and respect."

Humanity is at a crossroads. We have made great advances technologically, but we are facing deep problems that threaten our survival as a species. Until we recognize the importance of embracing the immutable laws of the universe instead of going against them, and until we can revere Nature as our ancestors did, the legacy we will bequeath to future generations will continue to compromise their survival. Let us find hope and inspiration in these pages, by learning the ways of the wise, as Timoté himself apprenticed to Cuatiendoy and shares now with us.

Alex F Crenshaw, MBA
Zen Institute
Mt. Shasta, California, May 2023

INTRODUCTION

Timoté, the central character of this narrative, describes how he unexpectedly met Cuatiendioy when he was only a high school student fleeing from the military, who were after him to punish him as a deserter for refusing to take part in a fight he did not consider his own, and ultimately for refusing to bear arms and kill his fellow human beings.

Cuatiendioy is a wise *Curaca* (someone in a position of authority and responsibility within his community) from the Amazon jungle, who rescues him from perishing in the jungle, baptizes him with the indigenous name of "Timoté," and entrusts him with the mission of conveying a message to the *civilized man.* At the same time, he helps him to find meaning in his life and teaches him how to heal long standing emotional wounds caused by painful experiences in his childhood. In the process, he also introduces him to the realm of physical healing by means of plants, and emotional healing with the essence of orchids

The *indio* Cuatiendioy is a wise man who has learned to navigate between two worlds. He has full knowledge of the needs of the indigenous peoples, and also understands the customs of what he calls *"the Civilized man,"* particularly his obsession with power and money, and his readiness to employ any means to obtain them. Cuatiendioy acts as a Messenger between the *Civilized man* and the *Indio,* and among the various indigenous peoples who still survive in the Amazon.

"Timoté" is a reproach of the intrusion perpetrated by our civilization and our technology against the essential world of the Amazonian indigenous peoples, together with the destruction of the foremost lung of the planet, with the cutting down of trees and the death of all the creatures living in it.

It is also a criticism of the indifference of governments towards the needs of the indigenous peoples who have been robbed of their resources and their way of life, as well as a denouncement of the impact of guerrilla forces and drug dealers, in areas that until recently, were free from the presence of the *civilized man*. It is also a portrayal of the indigenous peoples' struggle for survival, and their continuous efforts to move away from the "civilized" man harmful influence, only to discover that they have fewer places to go to, and fewer resources for survival.

In this narrative, readers will partly find a yearning for the old days and all the good things that are now gone. They will also find much hope for the attainment of a better quality of life, emotionally as well as spiritually, which may happen one day as a result of unexpectedly meeting another *Cuatiendioy,* who will help them to renew a connection with the best part of themselves, and to help heal the wounds inflicted by painful experiences in their pasts, thus enabling them to face the future with a lighter burden—just as the *Indio* still does and teaches us to do, living each moment impeccably, as he does, from moment to moment, deeply cherishing his clan, his family, his bonds of friendship, and above all, Mother Earth, with all her manifestations of life and with all the blessings she bestows upon us every day with the air we breathe, the water we drink, and the food we eat.

Nelson Valencia C.

CUATIENDOY

TIMOTE

I

Returning To The Moment Of Birth

"I can see strange things... I've just arrived. I feel slightly cold, wrapped up in the sheets. Back! I don't want to go! I want to know the reason for this arrival; I'm still crying, I can feel the dawn. The cocks are crowing and a candle barely shines some light in the darkness of the house. Someone whispers; 'It's a boy.' I am observing my own arrival... I can hear the goldfinches waking up, the mockingbirds, and the troupials, the voices of the laborers, the lowing of the cows. The courtyard is a festival of visitors and within the house, silence pervades the walls. 'Don't wake up the child.' I've just arrived from a long journey. Through the cracks of the protective doors, I can smell the fragrance of the coffee tree, of cow dung, of fresh milk and I see beams of sunlight mingled with shadows swaying with the wind. That's all I can see and feel, Cuatiendioy."

Cuatiendioy asked, "And what else can you feel?"

"Feel? I can feel the coolness of the morning and I can hear the sounds of the crickets, but I don't know why."

"Review you past," said Cuatiendioy.

"This is my past; I'm in it. What else can I search for?"

Cuatiendioy replied, "Go forward, then; we'll go along your path step by step together and don't forget the details; simple things can be the most important ones but you may miss them because they are so simple. I've brought you here so you can start looking for the clues to the meaning of life. Every man has a pathway, a reason for being here. If you examine your past, it's possible that you will easily find yourself.

"But the noise, forget the noise in your mind! When it appears, it brings confusion and leads you astray from your aim. Well, never mind now. I want to know what else you can see in your past today."

"I'm here. It's a sunny day. It seems there are several of us already; I used to hear them from inside my mother's womb; they're playing with mud in the courtyard. They're my two brothers, and the girl who glances at me out of the corner of her eye. It was her turn to play but I butted in; she doesn't accept me much, and I love her."

"Keep moving forward," Cuatiendioy urged.

"All right... It's a beautiful place! I can hear the river, very near the house. The house is built with sun-dried earth and straw (adobe) - my father calls them tapias; it's harvest time and there is a caravan of people arriving. There are women, too; they are singing as they come; their colorful costumes are beautiful, long gowns, scarves in many colors, and hats; they are all merry, they are lodging at the house on the cliff.

"Hanging from the laborers' waists are baskets where they put grain upon grain of the coffee tree harvest. There are many people; they come from distant places; some of them are acquainted with each other... A pair of blue eyes are looking inside me. There's something about them...they belong to a civilized man. It's don Emilio, a man who has my father's absolute trust. He is calm. There is something about his eyes... I want to see further beyond, but he's gone."

"It doesn't matter!" Cuatiendioy remarked. "You'll see him at some point. He's important to you; you'll find something else in his eyes. That's all for today. Let's wind this up and move on. We'll look for something to drink." And looking upwards, seeking out the sun amidst the thick foliage he said: "It's time to clean out our kidneys. We'll get water from the *lianas*. I hope you'll understand what I'm going to explain: if I cut the *liana* before you do, the water will quickly flow downwards and we won't be able to catch any of it. And if you cut it first, the water will go upwards so quickly that we won't have time to fill up a single *guaje* (a kind of sun dried gourd)."

He handed me a small knife and a *guaje*. Pointing to a vine, he ordered, "Cut it!" At the same time, he cut an upper portion of the *liana* himself. "Run! Fill up the *guaje!*"

I darted out, running through the thicket, carrying the *liana* on my shoulders, while a bluish, sticky liquid began spilling out from it. I filled up my *guaje* and at the same time, Cuantiendioy filled out his own *guaje* on the other end of the *liana*.

We drank the bluish liquid as we sat on the trunk of a fallen tree, and refreshed our kidneys with this marvelous beverage.

It was quickly getting dark in the jungle. I was anxious to find a hut or shelter, but he just continued to sit placidly on the fallen tree. I began to grow impatient wondering where we would be spending the night. It was the first night I would share with this strange man. So far, everything had been a bit weird. I still couldn't recover from the journey back to the moment of my birth, which he could so easily trigger by just touching a certain point on my spine. And he was sitting there, gazing at something more than the oncoming evening, and feeling something very different from the mosquitoes (which were certainly beginning to worry me).

"Timoté," he said. It's time to set up our *cambuche* (makeshift beds)."

"What!," I exclaimed. "Where are we going to sleep?"

"Right here! Can you think of a better place? This spot has accepted us. Can't you feel it?"

"I can't feel anything, not even my legs! We've been walking for so long, I don't even know where I am."

"We're both here, but your spirit isn't. *Become one with the moment!*"

"I don't understand what you're talking about. I just want to rest."

Cuatiendioy asked me to cut off some wide, crinkly leaves to make a raised bed with them, laying the large, cold leaves on a dry stockade, interweaving them one by one until they were left raised up as high as possible above ground level; I climbed up onto them and for an instant, I felt they were very cold, but when I snuggled under those leaves, a pleasant coolness spread over my whole body. I slept soundly to an extent I had experienced only on rare occasions at home.

I was awakened by a deafening noise in the morning; at the same time, I struggled with a total loss of any sense of time and space. I was overwhelmed with confusion and my heart was beating frantically; I had no idea where I was; hundreds of howler monkeys were screeching in fear at the sight of Cuatiendioy taking a leisurely walk amongst the trees as he conveyed his greetings to the morning. The echo was as sudden as a cry of alarm throughout the virgin jungle; later the pleasantly warm morning was made cheerful by the singing of the birds.

Still unsure of myself, I slowly got up, and walked amongst the lianas, fallen tree trunks, bushes and undergrowth, searching for some clearing free enough from the towering gigantic branches to allow some sunshine that would provide me with a bit of warmth.

Cuatiendioy was calm, relaxed; nothing disturbed him; he moved confidently, recognizing the environment, cutting off tender buds from some exotic plants. He observed the birds, the insects; it seemed as if I wasn't there, at least not judging by his eyes, which were oblivious to my stumbling and my struggle to make progress towards the ray of sunshine that filtered in through the jungle.

At one point, he crouched before a liana, seeming to be quite absorbed by it and totally ignoring everything else. I glared at him impatiently, yearning to coax him towards the place I was anxious to reach, but I didn't dare ask him how much longer we would be staying or who else we were waiting for. I knew he was fully aware of my uneasiness, and that he wasn't affected by it in the slightest.

After a while, he got up and said, "Look, that's what the parakeets eat. It would be a good way to start the day for you to collect a lot of it, because it seems it's all that we'll be eating today. We'd better not keep going until you can integrate better into the jungle. Let go of your haste. After all, we'll have all the time we need to continue moving forward.

"I don't know why you keep running all the time, Timoté. I haven't seen you being calm in any of the places where we've been; there is no calmness in your eyes, there is no calmness in your hands; your body isn't even calm when you're asleep. You look like fear walking within a sick body. I don't want us to continue our journey like this. I believe that, with all those frightened noises you carry inside, you will contaminate the jungle and she will devour you; she will eat you up like a hungry tiger. Bring some of those seeds the parakeets eat. We'll only eat what we need; you mustn't eat until you're completely full; just eat what you really need, as if to be ready to run if the jungle doesn't recognize you and gives you a scare. We haven't yet complied with our duty to ask the jungle for permission."

"What permission are you talking about, Cuatiendioy? How much more of the jungle do you want to see? All I care about is getting to some place where we can have a decent meal. Don't you think we're humans and need to eat different food from what the parakeets eat? I think we'd better turn back."

"You still keep on with your noises, Timoté. You'd better do as I tell you if you want to put something into your stomach that will provide you with real nourishment."

I walked over to the tree where the parakeets were serenely at rest and I gathered several berries; some of them had been pecked at and a smooth, reddish juice full of meaty seeds dripped out from them. I wanted to sit down and devour them right there, but I noticed Cuatiendioy was motioning me to come and sit beside him.

"Eat only four and keep silent; join me in keeping silent; keep silent with the jungle, and, most importantly, keep silent with yourself, so that you can slowly begin to merge with the jungle and we can continue our journey tomorrow. Watch the snail crawling on that leaf; just watch it and don't compare it with anything else; don't ask me anything; don't ask the snail anything either, or better still, become a snail yourself right now and eat at its rhythm. It will be better for your body and for the berry. The berry will become whatever you are thinking about: either food or poison."

I took four berries and sat beside him. Cuatiendioy had only one berry in his hand; his attention was fully absorbed by the berry, which was dripping its delicate juice down his fingers. He didn't seem to have the slightest intention of eating it. Instead he appeared to be in deep silent contemplation of it, as if the berry and Cuatiendioy were one.

Suddenly, in the midst of the deep silence, I felt the movement of the snail on the leaf; it was chewing on one of its edges. I could hear it and almost felt its subtle crawling. Lost in the scene, I heard Cuatiendioy biting into the berry he had been only contemplating a few minutes before. This led me to pick up one of the four I had placed next to me. Without losing attention on the snail, I bit the juicy berry. It instantly released a juice with such a special quality of sweetness that it pervaded all my senses. I forgot both Cuatiendioy's snail and the jungle itself. The fruit and I were one and the same thing; the juice on my hands and my own blood were a single source; the dripping juice was the universe; I was devouring the universe, biting off chunks of it.

I was wholly here, becoming one with the moment, my heart and the fruit, the jungle, one single mind, with nothing more to choose, nor wish to choose, nor anything to choose.

I ate up the four berries without realizing how long I took. Everything happened in a deep rapture; it was so strange that when I came back from the depth of that state, it was already late at night. I could tell by the croaking of the frogs, the chirping of the cicadas and the singing of the crickets.

The day had gone by more quickly than I expected. I didn't realize at which point I lost my sense of time, nor what could have happened for me to remain seated all day long to eat only four berries.

I turned to look at the snail. It wasn't on the leaf any longer. I drew closer, turned over the leaf it had fed on, and saw it resting unassumingly.

The sounds of the jungle made it clear that it was time again to set up our makeshift beds. The monkeys were gathering on the same tree. Their quarrels over the best spaces sent out a boisterous racket throughout the jungle. The parakeets were coming back from their extensive daily tours and were perching on the towering branches. The macaws would alight clumsily on the thicker branches, causing them to swing under their hefty weight, while each one of them used its sharp beak to fasten its grip on the thick branches and ceremoniously ensure its own space.

Suddenly, a sound similar to a swarm of bees rang throughout the scanty portion of sky which was barely visible through the tree tops. It was a cloud of bats. They alighted on the tree from which we had picked our berries. The tree was instantly covered in black and the jungle fell silent.

Cuatiendioy walked calmly around the tree where he had slept the previous night, and observed my disjointed movements. After going around the tree several times, he began to urinate around its roots, and bowed respectfully before climbing onto the leafy branch he had chosen. From there, he said, "Timoté, urinate around your *cambuche* -makeshift bed made of wide leaves"

I chose to ignore his suggestion, since I didn't feel the slightest need to urinate, and much less to go about spraying with my urine the area around my makeshift bed.

The night cast everything into darkness and in my fear, I covered up every inch of my body with leaves, with the only exception of my nostrils.

The sounds of the jungle gradually shifted from the boisterous chatter of the cicadas to the gentle singing of the birds, slowly bidding farewell to the day. Then came the subtle chirping of the crickets and the soft rustling of the armadillos as they passed by, the fluttering wings of the night moths, the sudden movements in the tree tops and the muffled sounds of nocturnal wanderers as they moved stealthily through the undergrowth. I felt everything was happening right next to my bed, as if all those creatures were spying on me from all over the place; and it even seemed some of them were so close that they were stopping by to sniff at my feet.

The jungle was in total darkness. I could no longer see the tree where Cuatiendioy was sleeping. I couldn't sense him making any movement either. I was beginning to sit up to try and catch his attention, when I heard his calm and reassuring voice. He said, "There are many sounds and noises, Timoté. You can't be drawn to all of them if you want to fall asleep. If you must seek outside, follow only the sound of the crickets. If you seek inside, follow the sound and the pulse of your heartbeats. Whichever of the two you choose, you'll be able to sleep peacefully."

So I followed the sounds of the crickets. In the pauses between the sounds and the silence, I fell asleep.

The next morning, there was a concert of birds greeting the day. A cool and welcome wind blew rhythmically over the gigantic treetops. As the trees swayed, large withered leaves dropped onto the ground below, forming a thickly padded carpeting throughout the jungle. Some leaves would drop randomly, alighting first on higher branches and gradually progressing downwards to the lower branches until they came to drop right on top of my improvised bed. The jungle awakened with the singing, chirping, and screaming of all the beautiful and exotic creatures: the bold ones and the helpless ones, the large ones and the tiny ones. The jungle was alive with a new song, a different sort of magic and rhythm.

In the midst of all these impressions, I could feel something near me, sniffing around my head. I sat up and saw a beautiful *lapa* (a small rodent, similar to a guinea pig) blending into the thicket. It began making its way towards the tree where Cuatiendioy was sleeping. It sniffed at its roots a few seconds and instantly moved on. Trying to keep track of its progress, I raised myself a bit more, leaning on my elbows, and began to draw up my legs to a sitting position. Right when I was in the process of beginning to do this, I felt a sharp movement amongst the leaves that were covering my feet. I stopped short, paralyzed by the sight of an enormous *Mapaná* snake taking up its position of attack. In a matter of seconds, it coiled back, raised its head and opened its jaws, exposing its sharp fangs and flicking its tongue. Its eyes were fixed on mine, clearly seeing me as its deadliest enemy. My breathing stopped. I was static, paralyzed and hypnotized by the snake's gaze, all in one second. A scream of sheer terror sprung out from the pit of my stomach.

"Cuatiendioy! Please help me!"

Cuatiendioy slept on the luxuriant tree I had seen him climb the previous evening. He had lain down between two huge trunks that resembled the shape of a hammock. I knew he was there, but I didn't dare look in his direction because it meant taking my gaze away from the snake, which was awaiting the slightest movement to dart at me and inject me with its venom, as deadly as a rattlesnake's or a cobra's.

In response to my cry for help, the snake made a brief backward movement with its head, as if taking impulse to attack.

Cuatiendioy's reply seemed to take an eternity in coming.

"Don't worry, Timoté! Everything's all right!" he replied calmly.

"It's a *Mapaná*... it's on my feet," I whispered.

"Don't move and let go of the fear. There's nothing to worry about."

"Cuatiendioy! Please help me!" I repeated.

"Don't worry. Everything's all right."

"What if it bites me?"

"If it bites you, you will simply die. You're scared and I know you want to turn to civilization for help. But do you know what this is? This is the Amazon. We are twenty days' journey away from the nearest town. And as you well know, the poison will act. In half an hour. you will no longer be on your feet. *Become one with yourself*! I've told you over and over again!"

"I don't even understand what you mean by that. But help me now and explain it to me later!" I retorted angrily. With every word that I struggled to pull out from my stomach and with the growing weakness in my muscles, I had the feeling the snake had drawn nearer. But it was actually static, as if casting a hypnotic spell on me, draining my strength, first from my legs, which I could no longer feel, and now from my voice, which drifted uselessly begging for help from a friend who was not making the slightest effort to help me.

"Well..." Cuatiendioy continued, "a *civilized man* will always run in one way or another, when he is faced with any danger or difficulty. His support is outside: in friends, in money, in liquor, or in so many other things that give him his false sense of security. The truth is that he rarely becomes a spectator of himself and of the circumstances around him. Look at you! You're about to shit your pants! I'm not asking you to use your power because the snake already has it. That is, it already has *you*. It *knows* it has you! It has absorbed all of your energy. Now the snake is the strong one and you're the weak one. Observe your surroundings. Realize what's going on!"

"I don't understand what you're talking about!"

"All right. Watch carefully and learn. That's the problem with trying to talk to people like you. You say you've been to school, and I don't know what school you're talking about. You need to understand that right next to each problem lies its solution. Only don't run. Become an observer of yourself and of your surroundings. Then you'll be able to see clearly. Seeing is not the same as looking. The snake is seeing you, while you just look at it. You need to see the snake and absorb its energy."

"I can't."

"All right. Start by looking at the tree and then try to *see* the tree where the snake is coiled."

"I can see the tree now, but the snake won't leave!"

"That's not my aim," Cuatiendioy insisted. "Very well, don't worry. I'll help you. *But you have to become one with the jungle. Otherwise the jungle will not protect you and you will die, so forget about ever going back home.*"

The snake was still there. It didn't shift from its position of attack. Without making the slightest movement, I was speaking from the deepest pàrt of my stomach with a companion who wasn't making the slightest effort to help me. I felt he was selfish, and a false friend.

I was about to burst into tears when I heard a gentle, whistling sound which came from Cuatiendioy's lips.The snake did not take its eyes off me, but when it heard the harmonious sound that Cuatiendioy had emitted, it closed its jaws, lowered its head, and started to slowly slither away through the underbrush.

A gentle sensation of warmth trickled from my cheeks down to my toes. Feeling free from the intense fear I had experienced, I regained control of my movements while I watched Cutiendioy calmly climbing down from his tree, with indescribable indifference, as if he didn't care whether I lived or died. Then he came close and said: "What a fool you are! A snake always sleeps near its antidote. This tree is the antidote. All you need to do is chew on one of its leaves and that's it. Get to know this well. Learn to have respect. You will have to ask forgiveness from the jungle for your thoughts. Killing the snake, indeed!

"What you need to understand about lethally poisonous creatures is that the deadlier their venoms, the better they are performing their role on this earth. They attract evil energies and turn them into poisons, which they then process and send down into the soil, transformed into different energies. (Later, I would come to understand that he was referring to the effects of radiation and of ultra violet rays)

"All right... get up and let's move on," Cuatiendioy urged.

"Today will be a very special day. We're going to look for several plants. We'll perform our duty of asking the jungle for permission. Then he asked, "So, you didn't do what I told you to do last night? You didn't urinate around the spot where you were going to sleep. After the scare you suffered, you'll learn to pay better attention to my words. We'd better ask for permission already. It's time for us to go deeper into the jungle."

After bowing respectfully to some of the plants, he cut off several branches while he performed his ritual dances and chants. He then cleared up some space, and formed a large circle with the branches. He instructed me to get into a smaller circle within the large circle he had just traced, Then he jumped into my circle. Turning his back on me, he said, "Listen! The plant calls us three times. We need to get closer every time. Otherwise, we'll miss it."

For an instant, it seemed as if the jungle had fallen silent at Cuatiendioy's command. All of a sudden, he jumped out and started running. As he did so, he urged, "Run! Run! it's near the *Ceiba* tree!"

Of course I hadn't heard anything. I just followed him. We stopped next to a beautiful *Ceiba*. He darted off running towards the left, just like a hare. I followed after him, still not hearing anything.

Then he shouted, "Second call!"

He walked slowly through the underbrush, in the manner of someone who is looking for something they have lost. I followed him close behind. We stood still for a couple of seconds. He closed his eyes. When he opened them again, he affirmed: "Here you are!"

He took a few more steps forward and right next to some leaves shaped like elephant ears, was the plant that, according to him, we were looking for. He drew near to it, walking in circles. He stroked its branches lovingly and then pulled out a small knife. He cut off several branches. He would chew on some of them and then cast them away. At one point, he handed me some leaves and instructed me, "Just chew on them and give thanks because the Ceiba doesn't always allow itself to be found. You'll soon see what we're going to do with this one."

We chewed some tasteless, sticky leaves and rolled them into little balls which we joined together, one by one, with a piece of fibre taken from a *liana*. We repeated the procedure until we had found about twenty plants.

Once we were done collecting the plants, we started searching for a bitter root called *yuko*. Cuatiendioy handed me one and told me to chew on it until I no longer felt hungry.

Then he said, "It's good for you to get used to it. It will be our best ally. Now we'll go get some water. We'll choose another ally. Go look for a *liana*."

I could see several *lianas* right in front of me. I pointed to them. "There are many right here. Which ones do you want me to cut off?"

"Not one of those! We'll look for a *liana* that will help you clean out the garbage you've been putting inside yourself in the city.

"Follow me. *White men* have no respect for themselves, and much less for the Earth. They consume all the garbage that is sold to them, without first examining its contents and the harm caused to their bodies. With their easy life, they poison themselves, they poison their own children and in the process, they poison the earth. Do you believe that the fear that has you in its grip has nothing to do with your poor kidneys, contaminated with that filth from bottled soft drinks and with deep rooted fears? Ah, but it's so easy to pop open the bottle and gulp down the contents in a flash. And we'd better not even mention the other garbage you eat. Just wait until your body is healed and you'll understand what I'm talking about.

"That *liana* over there is the one I want for you. I already explained how to do it so as not to waste this precious medicine."

He climbed onto the tree just like a monkey would, grabbing hold of *lianas* of different sizes and thicknesses. He sat on a branch that forked out from a huge trunk and tugged at a thick *liana,* bringing it down to the level of his forehead. He took his knife out of his backpack and counted up to three.

"Let's both cut the *liana* at the same time!" Then he urged, "Run! Fill up the *guaje!*"

I rushed out with the *liana* that was dripping with a bluish liquid. I filled up three *guajes.* Cutiendioy joyfully climbed down to drink the wonderful liquid.

He said, "This water is good for healing your kidneys. You need to drink up as much as you can of it before an hour goes by. After that, it's no use drinking it. Its healing power will be over and it will only be good for quenching your thirst. What matters now is that you heal your body so that you can see something more than physical objects using your eyes and see the true essence of everything around you.

By that time, I had already drunk up all the water from one *guaje* and had no problem in finishing them all, but Cuatiendioy had separated one for himself and with the calmness of a snail, he was sipping the wonderful bluish liquid. "We'll stay here. This is a good place to heal your body. There are many *lianas,* and it's about time we started your healing. Drink as much as you can. Pay attention to everything that comes out of you. I'll be handling what you need to put inside your body."

I continued drinking the water from the second *guaje* slowly, while Cuatiendioy kept on making comments about my eating habits. I felt uncomfortable. I wanted him to finish his speech so we could get on with the journey. But he just went on insisting that my eating habits had never been adequate. This only had the effect of triggering pleasant memories in my mind of all the delicious meals at my parents´ home I was missing. It also reminded me of the comforts of life in the city I couldn't enjoy, just because I was following this madman who dragged me into his strange world, where I neither belonged nor had any interest in belonging. But in the spaces between his comments and my distraction, there were beautiful moments of silence, when time lost its dimension and my body yielded to a temporary death with no effort or resistance.

Two hours of this ceremony had gone by. When I tried to stand up, I felt a sharp pain above my groin. I bent over and made a gesture that Cuatiendioy understood perfectly well.

"Don't move!" he urged.

"Finish up your *guaje*! Let go of your body! Your healing has already begun!"

"What healing, Cuatiendioy? I was healthy and you're killing me with this stuff you gave me."

The pain grew more intense. I was covered in a cold sweat. I was terrified something bad was happening to me. The pain clouded all my powers of reasoning. I cried out, "Cuatiendioy! I'm dying!"

"No, Timoté. You're being healed. The poison you've been taking in the past is coming out. Finish up your *guaje*, and let's wait."

The pain grew still more intense as Cuatiendioy approached. He took hold of my hands and held them in his. I clung desperately to them. His hands were bulky, coarse, calloused. In my agony of pain, I squeezed his hands tightly. He accepted it without the least resistance. Now his hands felt smooth and comforting. Their warmth made me feel reassured and for an instant, I felt I was a child being held in my father's arms The feeling of fear passed. I let go of his hands. I drank the last drop from the *guaje* and felt an overpowering need to urinate, together with a sharp, excruciating pain.

I stood up as best I could and tried to urinate, but the pain shifted down to my urethra. Unable to release a single drop, I started twisting and crying.

Cuatiendioy remained calm. Trying to reassure me, he said, "It will soon pass, Timoté. The poison is coming out. Loosen your body and the poison will come out easily. Observe your body."

His words reassured me. I could observe how tense I was, how rigid, fearful, with my jaws tightly clenched. I tried to loosen up a bit. I felt the pain below my kidneys again, and now I was able to urinate. I released a dark brown, foul smelling stream of urine. I lost count of how many stones came out as well, leaving my urethra with a painful burning sensation.

I felt the need to urinate again several times. After a while, my urine started becoming clearer and the pain was gradually less intense. The cold sweat disappeared. Exhausted, I lay down under a tree and fell asleep.

I don't know what else happened while I slept, nor how I got to my makeshift bed either.

The following morning, I woke up covered up with leaves and feeling as relaxed as if nothing had happened.

Cuatiendioy was there nearby, in calm contemplation of the morning. He could spend a whole day without moving, observing whatever captured his attention. This morning seemed to be one of those occasions. I got up slowly and sat next to him. I greeted him by just bowing my head. He looked me in the eye and then pointed to a praying mantis on a leaf. The mantis blended in so perfectly with its surroundings that it was barely visible. It was the same shade of green as the leaf was.

"Watch carefully, Timoté. We're going to wait for the message from the mantis."

Asking no questions, I watched the mantis closely. It did not make the slightest movement. But I didn't understand why I should spend so much time observing an insect that seemed to be petrified on a leaf. All of a sudden, it made such a swift movement that I didn't have time to catch sight of what happened. I could only see that the mantis was now holding an insect it had caught between its forelegs.

Smiling at me, Cuatiendioy said, "Waiting patiently is always worthwhile. Everything comes to you when you know what you're expecting. It's time to continue with your healing. We'll cut another *liana* before it gets too late and its healing color changes. Follow me. We're going back to the *lianas*."

We went back to the same spot where we'd been the day before. Pointing to a *liana,* he said, "This one is good for healing your intestines."

"I can't see any difference, Cuatiendioy. It's an extension of the same *liana* we used yesterday, and it's hanging from the same tree."

"Yes, Timoté. It's the same *liana* but this is a different time of the day. When I tell you, we'll cut it off just as we did yesterday."

He climbed up the tree and counted to three. We both cut off the *liana* at the same time. I filled up my *guaje* with a yellow liquid. I was sure it was the same *liana,* but the water had a different color.

"As you can see, it's not the same, is it? This water will heal your intestines, Timoté. It will cure you from all the filth you've always eaten. Don't worry about the color of the water. *Lianas* change color according to the time of the day. At different times its healing power changes. You mustn't think like a *civilized man* here. The *civilized man* doesn't know what things make him sick, and they all take the same medicine for the same ailment. They don't understand that we each of us have a different strategy to create our own sickness. That's why the cure has to be different in each case.

"The civilized man makes himself sick, in the same way that he makes the earth sick with the poisons he uses to try to kill his less evolved brethren. He kills himself. Every time he releases his poison to kill mosquitoes, he's killing his own children. Even his unborn grandchildren. The *civilized man* doesn't see what flows in his waterways. He can't hear the river weeping for its dead fish. He doesn't see there are less birds flying. He's wrapped up in his noises so he doesn't listen to his body either when it's being poisoned by the food he eats. You'd better drink this water before it loses its healing power."

"I don't want to go through the same thing that happened yesterday, Cuatiendioy. I don't want that excruciating pain again. I don't think I'm strong enough to bear it."

"There's nothing to worry about, Timoté. Come on. Drink this and we'll heal your bowels. They're more contaminated than the *white man's* waters and forests."

I drank the water slowly, more in response to Cuatiendioy's insistence than out of my own conviction. I felt nothing unusual.

Cuatiendioy stood up and said, "Well, Timoté, you've got all the jungle to yourself but don't pollute all of it. I'll leave you alone now so you can decontaminate yourself at leisure. I'll be back later." He turned around and disappeared into the jungle.

I felt scared of being alone. I tried to go after him but a bitter taste suddenly came up from my stomach and I was overpowered by the need to throw up. I bent over and vomited a thick, bitter slime. After intense activity in my bowels, I had bouts of extremely foul-smelling diarrhea all morning, I couldn't believe all that filth could have been inside my body. I got rid of so much disgusting stuff that I ended up feeling light, free from pain, and calm.

Cuatiendioy hadn't shown up yet so I sat down on a pile of dry leaves and started reminiscing about the time when I first met this man. I asked myself what I had been doing at the time.

I evoked the memory of a hot afternoon in a small village called Chicorodo -which means "Bamboo river". Chicorodo is next to a beautiful river that gives entrance to one of the most humid areas of the planet towards the Choco region and extending to the Darién region in eastern Panama. I was drinking a refreshing glass of *carambolo* juice (a tropical fruit) and while I stood next to the counter, I saw an *indio* who was coming in my direction. He was drenched in sweat and wore clothes that were unusual for that region. He was wearing white, baggy pants which came down to the top part of his calves, slightly below his knees and a black, loose-fitting shirt. Secured around his waist with a belt, he had a *jorongo* blanket. He wore sandals. His straight hair was cut with a rounded fringe which almost came down to his dark, penetrating eyes. An eye-catching feature of his mouth was a gold tooth coupled with a roguish smile. He was coming straight towards the shop, but his eyes were fixed on the glass of juice I was holding.

"My friend," I told him. "Have a glass of cool juice!"

"Thank you. I accept!" replied the *indio*.

I offered him a glass of the same juice I was having, the one he had fixed his eyes on. He drank it down quickly and then said, "Thank you, my friend! See you later!" and went off on his way.

At that time, I was a deserter from the army. I refused to fight for something I could not understand and I was terrified by the very idea of shooting at someone.

I was in my fourth year of high school. Colombia was in the midst of a crisis of violence and anarchy. Criminal gangs were beginning to infiltrate the government. University students often brought the country to a standstill, setting up roadblocks and throwing stones at the police to protest against social injustice. The government was taking over the whole country and handing the wealth out to a handful of families.

In retaliation for the protests, a curfew was imposed, which paralyzed the whole country at a given time of the evening. Nobody was allowed to go out into the streets. The military and the police were permanently patrolling in search of anyone they could find defying the prohibition. One afternoon, I inadvertently stayed too late in the school library. I was absorbed in reading a book by Friedrich Nietzsche and lost track of time. I didn't even realize that only a block away, all the students of my school were in a protest march clashing with the police, who had surrounded the university building and savagely beaten up every student they could catch. In solidarity with the university students, my schoolmates attacked the police with stones from behind their lines while the university students defended themselves throwing tiles they pulled off the roofs of their *alma mater*.

Meanwhile, at my school, all the teachers had left the building, and the silence was perfect for me to devour my book. I never knew how long the pitched battle went on. I only realized it was so late when Eutiquio, the school security guard, turned off the lights. He didn't notice I was still there. I stood up and shouted to him.

Eutiquio told me all about the recent events and indicated the safest way for me to walk home. I grabbed my schoolbag and set out on my way home, walking along the streets Eutiquio had suggested. The bus ride from the school to my house was about twenty minutes, but due to the curfew I had a one-and-a-half hour walk ahead of me. I had to avoid getting caught by the police or by the military. For the first forty-five minutes I walked safely, hiding every time I heard the sound of a car or saw some suspicious movement.

I had already left the downtown area behind me, and was feeling quite safe as I walked through the suburbs that were on my way home. But just when I was feeling safest, a soldier sprung out from a corner and in a thundering voice, he shouted, "halt!" I froze instantly. Aiming at my head with a huge rifle, he came nearer and ordered me to show identification. The moment he saw my student credential, without asking any further questions, he burst out shouting, *"Stone-thrower! Revolutionary!"* He took me to his truck. There were many other students there, guarded by several soldiers. He violently pushed me onto the back of the truck as if I was a sack of potatoes.

Many of the students were bleeding form the beatings they had received. Others were terrified and crying. We had no idea where the truck was taking us. They told us they were taking us to the garbage dump That was the place where dead bodies were found every day. They were the victims of the "Black Hand," which was a special branch of the police force who operated in civilian clothes and killed anyone who had been to prison more than once, for any crime. The military shared that same place when they had corpses to get rid of.

After several turns, we ended up in the Army General Headquarters, accused of being revolutionaries. We were held for two days in a dark cell, with no food or water. Finally, we were forcibly enlisted in the army.

We were "revolutionaries" sent out to kill "revolutionaries" who were in the mountains. The truth is that, although I was against the government and had made my position clear in public on many occasions, I had not been involved in any way with the protests this time. Nevertheless I was forcibly enlisted, briefly given military training and promptly sent out with my fellow recruits towards the mountains. Our mission was to hunt down any revolutionaries we could find. All my dreams were something of the past now. Ahead of me lay death, or the death of my fellow countrymen who were fighting to establish a different country.

One morning, the bugle call was earlier than usual. Right after breakfast, we collected our backpacks, hung our rifles on our shoulders, and climbed onto the trucks. We left the city behind with the vigorous efficiency of an army trained in a fratricidal war that had been going on for over fifty years.

The truck climbed up along the hostile mountain road, which carved its way amidst a landscape of menacing boulders. It seemed as if the boulders would break off and tumble down on us at the slightest movement. Slowly and stealthily, we took a narrow, single-lane dirt road. There was barely enough space on the road for the small cars the local guides drove. They knew all the hidden nooks where you could pull over to allow the passage of a car coming from the opposite direction. Ours was one of those local guides. He was formerly a peasant, now a soldier serving his country in combat, who owned a dilapidated 1954 Willys Jeep and had ample knowledge of the area. He had been captured and forcibly enlisted during an army raid once and was now entrusted with the mission of taking us to one of the most dangerous regions in the country.

It was hard to tell which was the greatest feat: to come out alive from those hazardous makeshift roads, or to survive an ambush staged by the guerrilla fighters, who knew better than anyone which were the strategic points where you could crush even the fiercest platoon.

We were all scared. The chances of getting back alive grew slimmer as the truck gradually left civilization behind and brought us into the dank jungle with a gloomy, thickly overcast sky above it.

We could hear the distant sound of a truck tooting its horn and driving along the opposite side of the road. We had to pull over and wait at the first spot where this was possible. Our driver tooted his horn as well and turned up our weak headlights, which only enabled us to see more or less three meters ahead through the darkness.

Taking advantage of the stop, we got off the truck to urinate. The most experienced among us unlocked the safety catch of their rifles and took up defensive positions. Rookies like myself climbed back onto the truck as quickly as we could to avoid the intense cold of the mountain.

When the civilian truck came to the spot where we were waiting for it, we stopped it and began to inspect its load. While we were doing this, the driver told our commander that he had already been intercepted by guerrilla fighters. He said they had requested a contribution for their cause and that they had taken several young men who were riding on his truck to enlist them as fighters in their revolutionary forces.

After hearing this, we realized that when we engaged in combat, we would either have to kill an innocent peasant, who was there against his will, or we would be shot dead by him in an absurd war.

There was a sudden change in our travel plan. Our unit was split in two. About twelve soldiers remained on the truck and fifteen of us set out on foot. We were to circle the mountain, keeping watch over the truck from above.

I was glad to be going on foot, under the guidance of an experienced commander who came from the coastal region. We gathered our weapons, ammunition, some survival gear and provisions and set out on our march downhill. Our truck driver had told us that the nearest village was three hours away. The guerrilla fighters were somewhere between us and the village, if they hadn't changed locations, which was by no means certain, since their strategies were unpredictable.

We had been walking for an hour or so, following the truck from our raised position. At that point, our commander made a change of plans. He ordered us to halt and said, "We're going to follow the truck from the low road on the left, bordering the river. If these bastards are capable of surviving in the jungle, they will be coming up along the river banks. It's the best way for them to cover up their tracks."

We set out again on the road he had indicated. I then realized that a battle was imminent. It would be the first time I shot at someone. Maybe that man would be shooting at me because he was being forced to do it, or maybe he would be convinced that by killing each other, we would change our country.

The irony of it was that I was also in favor of having a new government that would bring more justice for all. Political leaders in the government always manipulated the people into believing that the guerrillas were the problem.

It was very convenient for them to blame the guerrillas while the country was being sold out to multinational corporations, hunger was rampant in the streets, indigenous peoples were not acknowledged as citizens and laborers of African descent were still being treated like slaves in the banana plantations.

However, none of my reflections were relevant when my life depended on the outcome of a battle that would start at any moment now. I knew there was fear in every single one of my fellow recruits. They were as scared as I was, or even more so. We moved forward stealthily, along pathways leading to the river we needed to cross. We were heading for a vantage point from which to cover our truck when it came to the last curve in its descent from the mountain.

But the guerrilla fighters had devised a strategy that would enable them to wipe out the whole platoon at once. From that fateful curve in the road, where the olive green color of the truck blended with the green hues of the jungle, a deafening explosion reverberated far and wide, and grey smoke - as grey as death - filled up the air with pain and anguish. Before the last piece of metal wreckage had fallen back onto the ground, the more experienced soldiers in our platoon let loose a barrage of bullets against the guerrilla fighters, who were unaware of our presence at their rear.

The massacre on both sides took only a second. When I tried to jump onto a rock that would allow me a clearer view of the enemy, I fell into the rushing waters of the river. The turbulent current carried me swiftly away, as if I were a mere leaf in a roaring outburst of violent floodwater that drags away anything standing in its path.

In a flash, I saw my whole life unfolding before me like a film projected on a screen. Every time the river would allow me to come to the surface for air, that moment of breathing felt like the rest of my life to me. The second challenge in my hideous struggle for survival was awaiting in the muddy whirlpools near the river mouth, where I scored my second victory over death.

I was almost naked. I'd lost most of my clothes. I rescued some of the military gear that was still floating in the huge whirlpool and scrambled into the mountainous wilderness like a frightened deer. After two days walking, I came to a small village where I was kindly received and cared for. The villagers clearly thought I was mentally ill and treated me accordingly. This was due to my physical appearance. My pants were torn and I wasn't wearing a shirt. Since it was part of my military uniform, I'd been forced to leave it in the same hiding place in the bush where I'd left my rifle. It was in that village where I first met Cuatiendioy.

I was immersed in my reminiscing when Cuatiendioy appeared with some new plants. He placed them on the trunk of a fallen tree. He cut off a branch and used it to trace a circle around the plants he had gathered. Then he started giving thanks to the jungle. After that, he took out a kind of gum from his backpack and mixed it with the plants. The result was a greenish sticky goo. He rubbed his face with it, as well as his neck, arms and legs. Then he handed me the concoction and said, "Here! Rub some of this on your skin before the swarms of mosquitoes start arriving."

I was applying the mosquito repellent on my skin when he took out something else from his backpack. He handed me a small green bag and said, "Keep this garlic amulet in your backpack and you won't come across a snake ever again."

He added, "Judging from what I can see, your intestines healed well. How do you feel now that you're free from all that filth?"

"I'm fine. Just a bit tired and weak. How else would I be?"

"I want us to continue with your process. This *ceiba* tree has room for all. Today there will be two more of us. Let's earn our space on it. Feel! This *ceiba* accepts us. I think you're lighter now and can begin to feel it. At least, your body is not so contaminated. We'll see about your spirit later. From now on, you need to be careful with what you eat. You mustn't contaminate it with your thoughts."

I looked closely at the *ceiba's* luxuriant, embracing arms. It took some effort to reach one of them where I could settle comfortably while life in the jungle was gradually winding down for the end of the day. I pulled out my notebook and a pen, and was overcome, for the first time in my life, by a feeling I couldn't explain. Something sprung up from the depths of my heart and contemplating the beauty of that tree, words I couldn't hold down began flowing out of me. So I wrote:

Before me, the tree...
sentry of the wind.
Dancing to a rhythm,
static at times,
indifferent to the world,
weeping dry leaves as tears
harboring flights,
concealing insects,
sending out bird offspring,
stretching out its neck,
casting shade on the bushes,
cooling the ground below,
warily, it watches me.
Standing upright, it awaits.
A hundred thousand green hairs
land at my feet
from its charmed crown
which, swaying to a gust of wind
for no reason at all,
lurches out.
The tree rains on me,
welcomes me, speaks to me.
Tough am I with the unfolding of the world.,
with thirst, with the rain,
with the wind,
with tremors,
with wild beasts,
but weak with man.
Please, do not cast me down!

Cuatiendioy was watching me in silence. When I had finished writing my last word, he cried out, "Not yet! You've barely begun to feel and already you want to make marks on everything, set limits on everything, compare everything, say everything! Listen, Timoté! It's better to go back to the beginning. First things first! You already have one clue. If you find the rest of them, you'll understand all of this and more One day, you'll write about all of this. I'll tell you when! Climb down, Timoté. We'll continue with your search.

"Relax again, surrender to the embrace of the jungle, and you'll understand more than this. Listen!" Pressing down with his fingers on some points in my spine, he took me back to my childhood.

"How old are you, Timoté?"

"I'm seven years old."

"What do you see?"

"I'm harvesting vegetables with my mother: tomatoes, onions, beets. I can smell the whole kitchen garden. I'm happy in this place! Daddy told me we'll go fishing tonight. I'm waiting eagerly for nighttime. I'm looking at my mother. I never noticed her eyes were so sad. I understand why. My older brothers aren't here. My father decided they had to go live in the city. I don't know what the city is. My older brother, who lives there, has told me stories about it, and shown me movies. My father has also told me stories. It's his custom to gaze at the sky every evening. When night falls, he gazes at the moon and the stars. He takes me in his arms, holds me tight, and we begin to feel the universe and its silence. He speaks to me about it. I hadn't noticed. I'm feeling. I can see and clearly hear the rhythm of his heart. Every afternoon we travel together all over Europe when he reads to me. When we read about Nero, we go to Rome. Then we are captured by the silence of the night.

"I understand clearly now, Cuatiendioy, the reason why I love afternoons. It's because I can feel my father's silence in them. I also understand why I love the soil. I am feeling it now that I can see those fresh vegetables I'm harvesting together with my mother. I can hear her voice...

"'Look, son!' my mother is saying, 'how beautiful the earth is. It's sad to think there are so few men who respect it!'

"My mother is feeding the chickens now. She's always busy. Sometimes she prays.

"I'm looking forward eagerly to this evening. It's the day my father goes fishing. It'll be the first time I go with him. We're walking along the narrow pathway that leads to the river. My father has something to tell me. There's something happening that affects us both.

"'Listen, son,' my father says. 'You're already seven years old and you need to go to school.'

"My father wants to push me away too and I can't accept it. I don't want to fish anymore! I want to go home! I don't understand!"

"That's all for today. Don't get lost," Cuatiendioy said. "Let's go to sleep now. But first, search for silence. Don't forget the details of this experience.

"You were able to see each day and every detail clearly. Now, look at this evening. It's your very last evening. There will never be another one like this one, nor will I be around to remind you of it.

"It dies, Timoté. Yesterday dies, tomorrow dies. The spirit of the evening is only present in this moment. The wind, the falling leaves, you and I. We are also the evening. We are its spirit. There is no distance. There is no time. There is no tomorrow. We mustn't allow this moment and its eternity of minutes to escape from us. Don't get entangled in your mind, thinking that tomorrow will be better. Don't waste your chance of experiencing the intensity and the magic of this evening."

"I'm sleepy," I told him. And trying to gaze at a star through the swaying foliage, I fell asleep.

II

The Calls From The Jungle

The next day I was awakened by the singing of the jungle, just like every morning. The first thing I did was to look for Cuatiendioy. He was in a sitting position, his backbone upright. He seemed as if he had slept in that posture. His eyes were open, unfocused. I tried to catch his attention but he was oblivious to my efforts. I observed him for a moment, without asking him anything. I tried to understand his silence. At one point, he shifted his head towards me. He fixed his black, penetrating, shiny eyes on me, as if at the same time, he were seeing into the depths of my soul and said, "You make more noise than the howler monkeys, Timoté. Bring your mind to stillness! This is and will be a beautiful day. Today we'll be moving forward still further. I must tell you there will be experiences. The rains are coming. They will last long, and we will have live with them."

"But how? Where will we find shelter?"

"Right within it!" he replied. "Isn't it the same rain as the deer's, the bird's or the tiger's?. It's the same for all. *Become one with this!*"

"All right. Where are we heading to?"

"To find your past and in it, some clues about your life."

"What clues? I didn't know life had clues. I've never heard about this before. Neither at school or at home. What do you call "clues?" And what else can I find in my past? Besides, who cares about the past. After all, it's gone already."

"Maybe you'll remember something from the past that you can heal, and when it is healed, it may help you if you go deep into silence, Timoté."

"I'm tired of memories. Why would I want to suffer remembering my painful past?"

"So that you can be free from all the aches and pains in your body. So that you can straighten up your slouching posture. So that you can empty your mind a bit and become one with this moment. Can't you see that your memories never stop haunting you? They prey on you in all those parts of your body where you feel pain. If you can't understand yourself, how can you understand me, and understand the jungle? To begin with, become one with the rain and you won't need to come back some day to search for the clue of this moment, that is to say, the meaning of this moment. Every instant, every event, no matter how simple and insignificant it may seem to you, has its purpose. Without forcing yourself, you must try to see the meaning of those events, and find the magic that lies within them. Let's get going."

We walked in silence through the thick, dank jungle. There was a boisterous band of monkeys and parakeets fleeing in the same direction, which was opposite of the one we were heading for.

Cuatiendioy stopped and taking a look at the birds, he said, "It's going to be a beautiful storm. We will share the moment with it and merge with it!"

Just as he was speaking, it started raining harder. I took off my clothes, including my boots and socks and put them in my backpack. All I had brought were two pairs of pants, two shirts, five underpants, six pairs of socks, my note book, pens, pencils (and a compass, which, by the way, I never used or even needed). What I did have were numerous herbs. We had gathered them during our constant searches. We would roll them up into tiny balls which we fastened to one another in a way that made them look like a sort of rosary. We carried them around our necks.

I walked happily in the rain, chewing on some leaves that were as bitter as absinthe. It was not too cold and I wasn't even afraid of catching a cold. I wasn't hearing my mother's voice any longer. She always used to warn me when I was a child, 'Watch out with the rain, you can catch a cold'. At the slightest contact with rain, I would come down with a flu. Here I was breaking free from that conditioning. Cuatiendioy was enabling me to walk in the rain without any consequences. Except my sense of completeness.

We walked more than ever before and stopped at a beautiful spot. We cut off some branches, stuck them securely into the ground and joined their tallest ends together, forming a kind of *igloo* or *temascal* hut. After we had lit the fire, we sat down to consider it. Cuatiendioy started walking in circles around the *temascal* in order to protect our dwelling. While he was doing this, he instructed me, "Straighten up your backbone. Align your ears with your shoulders. Don't move so much. Pay attention to your eyes. Remember that your eye movements will determine your thoughts. Leave the fire as it is. Fire changes. Withdraw your gaze and observe the dry leaf you have right in front of you. Look closely at it with your eyes open until you no longer see it. Only then will you become a leaf and if you can become a leaf, you will also be able to become a wild boar, a cougar, a snake, a monkey, an eagle, a condor. What I'm saying is, don't measure it with your thoughts. Don't bring it into your mind as the civilized man. Watch the leaf closely and let your thoughts flow freely. Go deep into the silence but don't cling to the idea of finding it. It comes when you stop measuring, comparing and judging everything you see, hear and touch.

"You need to understand that your mind is caught up in all that white men's stuff. That's why your mind is lost. You'll see that without things to provide you with entertainment, there is no mind. You will then know what there is in emptiness. There's nothing there, Timoté. But it's a nothingness that will bring you much peace. Then you'll be able to sit under a tree and that tree will be your universe. Until the tree and the jungle cease to exist, you will continue sitting there with your mind blank. Sit down and breathe. You need to enter the non-existence of the tree, and to understand the no-mind of the *indio*."

"How can you say that, Cuatiendioy? This tree exists even when I am not here. This jungle has always existed and would exist even if I had never come here."

"This tree and this jungle begin to exist now for you, Timoté. Their true existence is in becoming one with you. Otherwise they will exist only in your mind through the things you measure and touch, and through the things you compare with the world you have known: the civilized man's world. Your mind cannot grasp the essence of the jungle. It's looking at shapes, searching in the noise the monkeys make. White men look at the jungle in little pieces at a time. They don't contemplate the calmness of the tree. Actually they see it transformed into chairs, doors, windows, firewood. As regards all the rest of life that is found in the jungle, they hunt it down to cage it, mistreat it, to humiliate it in their confined spaces that are a reflection of their incapacity to become one with the Life that gives them life.

"What will happen, Timoté, when there are no more *Guacamaya* birds in the jungle, when the *Tití* monkeys are gone forever? They will disappear, just as the condor, that great messenger, is being eliminated by the *civilized man*. The clean waters will also disappear and the tree that is killed here every day so the *civilized man* can turn it into tables and other objects that give the *civilized man* a sense of meaning to his existence. They have no respect even for their own lives.

"Well, Timoté. We won't continue with this topic, now. Let's carry on with your healing. I want to let you know that we'll be having visitors tonight. We need to make a covenant with the jungle. The warmth from our bonfire will attract them. But you'll learn to get along with all of them. You'll see. In spite of this mess we cause by making a bonfire, there will still be order. We won't be disturbing anything if we remain calm and respectful with all our curious visitors. No creature will have the power to upset you, no matter how strange its appearance may seem to you. You mustn't have thoughts about killing. Respect for life is foremost. Keep calm all the time. Don't underestimate the smaller creatures either. And above all, mark out your space."

By then, my mouth was already watering with the need to have something warm to drink. I was feeling cold and my body was craving for warmth. I needed some tea or something to warm my hands and my body. As if he had read my mind, Cuatiendioy pulled out a piece of bamboo he had among his things. He had carefully cut out a small slice of it to make a kind of pot. With the remaining smaller portion of bamboo, he had made an original cooking utensil. He filled the pot with water, added some plants and aromatic herbs and covered it tightly with its seamless lid, which in turn, he covered with mud. He placed the pot on the embers and we waited for a few minutes. He then pulled the bamboo pot off the embers. It was hot by now. He carefully removed its lid and a pleasant smell came out of the pot and spread all over the *temascal*. Finally he took out a small, amber colored jar which contained a sweet, transparent liquid.

"This is *jimeirta* bee honey," said Cuatiendioy.

"What kind of honey, did you say?" When I was a child, we had always used honey as an indispensable component of our diet, and *angelita bee* honey as eye medicine. The name *jimeritas* was totally unknown to me. So I said, "I'm well acquainted with bee honey, which is thicker than this one. I don't know what *jimeritas* are."

"You'll soon see. They are very tiny bees. The best allies in my journeys. They don't sting, and they are my noblest sisters in the jungle."

He added a bit of honey to the contents of the bamboo pot and poured out the delicious tea into two dessicated gourds. He held one of them in his hands and delicately handed it to me, as if it were a treasure. Then he picked up his own cup and sitting in his habitual cross-legged lotus position, he fell silent.

We drank the tea. I had never tasted anything so delicious in my life. I had never experienced before the intensity of enjoyment my body felt, to the point that I wished it would never end. I felt as if every single one of my cells was opening up to taste this beverage, and then closed up again to capture this marvelous energy. It was simply a time to enjoy tea in the middle of jungle. Everything contributed to my becoming one with Nature. *This feeling brought back to me some experiences with my father, such as when sometimes on rainy days, he would invite his laborers to have a cup of the coffee they had harvested. They all came in silence, as one does at a ceremony. My mother would put a large pot with water and brown sugar on the fire and when the water boiled, she would add the freshly ground coffee. The house was pervaded with a delicious fragrance. All the guests came out from their rooms in response to it. They had just finished taking their showers and still had the fresh smell of soap on them. They created a gallery of fragrances, amongst which the coffee was predominant. They would sit in a circle, each of them drinking their cup of hot coffee, sitting silently, just as my father liked it. It was a ritual, a sacred moment, and sometimes my mother would take advantage of the occasion to start a prayer. To be sure, whenever she had conversations with anyone, my mother never missed a chance of trying to persuade them of how important it was to be at peace with God. My father had a very silent God. He never spoke of Him, but every evening he would gaze into the sky as if he were looking for Him amongst the clouds, or trying to find Him on some star. Coffee-times were sacred to me, because I had more time to be in my father's arms, while I shared that moment of silence with him.*

Now in this present moment, I realized I experienced a similar feeling, regarding this enigmatic man. I felt I had nothing to worry about and that I could remain there forever. I could even die. My entire body was filled with a feeling of peace. There was nothing I wished for, nothing I needed. This dwelling built with sticks and leaves was a grand mansion. Or a tiny heaven floating over the jungle.

We finished our tea. Cuatiendioy remained sitting, with his backbone completely upright, his eyes half-open and gazing ahead. He seemed to be abstracted from everything or immersed in everything. His presence was indescribable.

I tried to catch his attention but nothing affected him. I wanted to understand his silence. I copied his posture, straightened up my spine just as his was and let go of the rest of my body. I briefly imitated his breathing, remembering that he had sometimes encouraged me to imitate the movements of a monkey or some other animal saying, "Imitate and you will obtain an identical result." At that moment I was imitating him, trying to attain his silence.

I surrendered to the sound of the crickets, which gradually faded away and I made contact with my breathing, following his, and again I felt immersed in a feeling of peace. His previous teachings kept appearing in flashes: "Attain my stillness but don't seek for your stillness in my silence. If you do, you'll always be seeking outside. And there is nothing outside of yourself. Then you'll go back to the *civilized man's* thoughts and you'll continue being lost. You can't understand this because you can't stop your thoughts. You're already creating stories to find better entertainment, and you get caught up again in what you're thinking."

These words were alive in my mind and became more vivid with my stillness. They came to me with greater clarity of understanding. I was able to realize that I had rarely paid attention to his teachings. Or to be honest, never.

Now that my mind was still, his words came to me like flashes of lightning.

"Become a leaf, Timoté. Become the wind. Become an insect. And jump into the void being as light as a leaf. Attain the mind of the *indio,* who is leaf, cricket, river, drop, cloud, and nothingness. You are leaf, you are cricket, you are wind. Once you have understood this, you will understand how simple we are in life. But don't try to attain the mind of the *indio* without first finding peace in your own mind.'

I turned my eyes towards Cuatiendioy and his gaze met mine. I had never seen his eyes so alive and penetrating. He was seeing inside of me. I felt it. It seemed as if he was looking into my soul.

He stood up and coming towards me, took out a small *guaje* from his backpack. It had a strange and pleasant fragrance, which was a mixture of flowers and *cundú* roots (a plant to which Cuatiendioy's people attribute magical and healing powers). He rubbed me with it and said, "It's to make sure you won't be distracted by anything, not even the mosquitoes."

He walked back to his place, took up the lotus sitting position again and fixed his gaze on the last flame of the fire, which was already beginning to die out. From where I was sitting, I began to follow his breathing closely, observing the almost imperceptible movements of his chest. I felt I was floating in the midst of an immense silence. For the first time, I entered into a void that was detached from everything. To this day, I still can't find words to describe this feeling. In fact, I don't know whether such words exist in our language, or in any other language.

There were two other moments in my life when I had something similar to this experience. The first one was in a Zen temple near Sakura-shi, Japan. The second one was in a Zen meditation center in Cuernavaca, Mexico. Some day I will share those experiences.

The last flame had died out, and only the embers and the concentrated warmth persisted. Dew drops fell from the trees, gently striking the dry leaves. In the depth of my silence, I could feel I was a drop, I was rain, *liana,* leaf, wind.

I don't know how long we remained sitting in that position. I found it was truly comforting although I wasn't accustomed to it. Following Cuatiendioy's breathing, everything else became unimportant. I felt time go by swiftly and had no sensation of my body. It was all very pleasant until I made contact with my body again. At that moment I was overcome with a sharp, overwhelming pain that I could feel in the uttermost portions of my body.

I managed to start moving very slowly and gently. Little by little, the aches subsided. Then I began to feel curious about Cuatiendioy's thoughts. I wondered where his mind was. I asked myself what his movements would be upon recovering contact with his body after sitting in the lotus position for so long. He remained sitting, motionless, in a lotus posture, with his eyes half-closed, immersed in the depths of a void in which everything seemed pervaded by profound nothingness.

I interrupted his silence to say, "Is there any more tea left?"

"No. When a good thing is scarce, it is all the better for being scarce. Never forget that."

Then he went back to his sitting posture and remained silent.

My weariness proved stronger than my curiosity. I snuggled up and surrendered myself to the night and found a special charm in it. I didn't know whether it was the tea, or the experiences shared with Cuatiendioy, who had a new surprise each day, a plant with a new story. In my dream he would appear, repeating his phrases so vividly that I could no longer distinguish between the dream and reality. Drawing close, he would speak into my ear, "While you are more asleep than you usually are, I want you to understand that if the *civilized man* does not penetrate for a second into the essence of the jungle, he will never defend it, he will never love it because he will see it as something remote and different from himself. Only when there are no trees left, or rain, or deer, or *lapas*, when the cougar and the wild boar have nowhere to hide, the *civilized man* will also find that he has nowhere to go either, nor water to drink, nor shade from a tree to lie under. The *civilized man* will sit down to weep over his life wasted in a frantic search for something that will never bring him fulfillment.

"Embrace the tree, Timoté. Ask it to forgive you for the ignorance of the *civilized man*. After all, you're a *civilized man* yourself and you're as guilty as they are for what is being done to the Earth."

In my dreams, I tried to embrace the tree, but it drew away from me, leaving me with a feeling of anguish that after a time would vanish when I fell into deep sleep.

When I woke up, I looked towards the place where Cuatiendioy slept, but he was no longer there. He was coming with water to prepare a different tea. Without saying a word, he brewed the tea with his usual enthusiasm for the task. Although it was delicious, it lacked the special charm of the tea we had drunk the night before.

"Cuatiendioy," I asked. "How do you manage to remain in a sitting position all night?"

"How do you manage to be asleep all the time?" He retorted.

After a pause, he said, "Let's go, Timoté. This day will bring new delights. The winds will be changing direction. There will be rain, but it will be warm in the daytime. There are messages from the jungle deep inside. There will be a felling of *ceibas* trees. I dislike those blackened spaces, those scars in the jungle. We all pay the consequences for them. We'll have to look for short cuts to get there and sense the reaction of Mother Jungle. Get your things. We'll give thanks to this beautiful space for the hospitality we were shown, and then we'll be on our way."

I did as he instructed and gathered the few things we were carrying with us, while Cuatiendioy bowed in the direction of each of the cardinal points, giving thanks to the environment as one does when bidding farewell to a friend.

We set out, following the echoes Cuatiendioy could hear. To me, it was as if he were listening to the weather forecasts or to the the news on the radio. It was the first time I could tell this man was worried, I could hear it in his voice. So I asked him, "Please explain, Cuatiendioy. Who told you something? Is there anyone out there? Who did you talk to?"

"What a fool you are. What did you come for? Didn't you say you were here because you wanted to get to know the Amazon jungle? Of course, now I see it. You're just like those *white men*, those who speak with complicated words and bring cameras and strange equipment. They look around at everything, they walk about saying they are getting to know the Amazon jungle but they don't feel anything. They don't see anything. They just come to bring us their fears and to pollute the sacredness of this space, the only innocent space on Earth. Did you notice the birds as we were walking into the jungle? They're already scared. And so are the wild boars, the raccoons and the deer. Fortunately, we're going to a place the loggers haven't reached yet. They won't get to our sacred space. There's going to be a falling of ceibas. Adapt your way of walking to mine."

III

Seeking For The Honey Of The Jimeritas

And we set out on our journey. I walked behind, following Cuatiendioy through a cloud of mosquitoes that darkened the sky. The luxuriant and shiny *ceibas* cluttered up the scarce patches of sky. They swayed more gently as we walked among them, and the warm afternoon wind blew on our faces, bringing the fragrance of damp earth from far away.

An infinite silence floated in the thicket. The only sign of our presence was the crackling of the few dry leaves when Cuatiendioy would step on them. Cuatiendioy moved forward like a warrior in search of his prey: confident, his posture erect, as if there were no obstacles in his path. I walked behind him, with my noisy baggage of fearful thoughts, struggling to avoid losing sight of him in the dense jungle.

In the afternoon, we already began to hear the echoes of the chainsaws, the noises of the loggers, the boisterous stampede of the monkeys as they passed high above our heads, scared away from the first trees that had been cut down. The jungle moaned with pain as the first *ceibas* fell down with a thundering roar.

Bewildered, holding his head in his hands, Cuatiendioy exclaimed, over and over again, "Poor jungle! What will your reaction be?"

We came to the place where the loggers' camp was. We climbed a tree and through its foliage, we caught sight of the beautiful, shiny *ceibas*, so ancient that if a logger were to plant the seeds for new *ceibas,* not even five generations would be enough for us to see such beauty again. And there they were, awaiting death, at the hands of ignorance. Life that had developed for over three hundred years was about to be destroyed, just as anything else that stood in the loggers' way.

"There they are!" Cuatiendioy hissed. "They are always the same ones. Look at the squalor they live in here, and wherever they go, because squalor is always with them. We will ask the jungle for permission on behalf of the loggers to cut the ceiba trees, for they are only receiving orders from the logging companies that exploit them. We will also ask her to help them understand the damage they are inflicting on themselves every time they cause harm to the jungle."

We climbed down from the tree. Cuatiendioy gathered some branches and traced a circle on the ground. He began dancing within the circle, while uttering guttural chants. With the rhythm of his body movements he imitated the clouds, the wind and the water. After that we collected some sticks and leaves to build a makeshift place to rest in. Later, a violent storm broke out, and it rained all night long. Cuatiendioy said thoughtfully, over and over again, "it's the rage of the jungle, Timoté. It's the rage."

Large quagmires were formed all over, and the next morning everything was flooded. There were only a few islands of higher ground to be seen, like the one we had settled on. Surveying the quagmires, Cuatiendioy said,"The mosquito clouds will be arriving soon. With them, malaria will come. The revenge of the jungle. It's time for us to leave, Timoté."

And so we left, on a damp morning. The sun was timidly filtering through the thick jungle. Sometimes, the scant rays would alight on my head for a few seconds. Cuatiendioy began to walk faster. He avoided the swamps and found pathways that led us away from the flooded areas. We crossed streams on makeshift skiffs made with sticks tied up together with *lianas*. We walked on like zombies, forming part of the same stampede as the howler monkeys. They with their noise out in the open, and we with the screaming within ourselves.

After several hours of walking without uttering a word, Cuatiendioy stopped and said, "Listen! There are new calls from the jungle."

"Who is it calling to?"

"All of us," he replied. "Anyone who feels they are a child of the earth. All those who enjoy being on her, and who know that what they breathe is hers. All those, Timoté, who listen to her spirit."

"How is that?"

"Look, Timoté. The earth is alive. It moves and breathes. It's a body that is alive. She walks, with us upon her. We travel on top of her. Some of us like monkeys, making noises. Others like snakes, crawling on the ground. Some like eagles, watching from above. And others like mosquitoes, the kind you can't shake off and are too much of a nuisance.

"There are things that annoy the earth just as there are things that annoy your body. Your body is matter and spirit, and they both seek harmony. When you have a cut on your finger, doesn't your whole body feel it? Everything in you moves. Even the tiniest part. Everything has an order. If this order is altered, your body gets sick. There's an order here also, a spirit who moves the earth. And there is no difference. The earth is a body, different from yours, only as long as you see it that way.

"Just as the *civilized man* can shorten distances and speak from different locations, the earth is also able to communicate. When a *ceiba* falls here, struck down by a man, its echo, its effects, are being felt in every corner of the earth. She gets sick. The *civilized man* makes her sick. If only you knew, Timoté. Water sometimes falls here, other times it falls over there and when it is altered here, it is being altered over there. This water is the same for everyone. One drop knows what is happening to the *civilized man's* water, the *indio's* water, and the ocean's.

"Some day, the *civilized man* will understand what the *indio* has learned from the spirit of the earth. The *indio* sees beyond shapes. The *civilized man* sees the surface. He doesn't understand his own life, and much less can he understand other people's. He lives for himself and doesn't care about the harm he is causing his own children, his grandchildren, and the earth. The *civilized man* causes our flowers to wither so that his own flowers may live. But even with his living flowers, he has no time to perceive their fragrance. He seeks for gold in everything. In fact, he seeks for everything in the external world. When his time comes to wither and die, he realizes he has lived sitting on top of a treasure (life), and finds no peace. In other words, he lost the gold mine and has to leave this world anyway. But none of that matters unless it is understood inside oneself.

"The *civilized man* will pay a high price for not respecting the spirit of the earth. One day, everything he seeks in the outer world will turn against him and suffocate him. Then he will pay attention to the simple things in life because they will enable him to find its meaning. Don't fill yourself up with *civilized man*. Fill yourself up with *indio*. Even though you may think my sandals are ugly, they're all my feet need when I want to enter the *civilized man's* world. But believe me, Timoté, I don't like the noise in which the *white men* lives. Seek for silence, and learn to understand the *indio's* world."

While he kept on talking to me about his world, I began to feel I couldn't keep up with this swift strides, and said, "I'm worn out."

"Model your footsteps on mine. Follow my rhythm," he replied.

I tried to catch up with his strides, which seemed as if his legs were being pushed from behind by a gentle wind. For an instant I felt as if I were floating, or as if obstacles were shifting aside to make way for him to pass. I walked faster and tried to step on the same places where he had stepped, but it was useless. I felt all sorts of obstacles cropping up to hinder my feet. The more I tried to catch up with him, the further ahead he seemed to be. He was like a shadow floating over the marshes or a ghost swinging on the tree branches. I realized it was no use trying to keep up with his rhythm so I surrendered to my own rhythm and forgot about his footsteps. I gave up struggling to catch up with him and just followed my own breathing. I felt we were very close to each other because I could hear his heartbeats, although I couldn't see him. Far ahead on the path I could see branches that were partially flattened where he had trodden on them as he moved forward, but I felt we were breathing at the same rhythm. I felt as if his heart and mine were one. I began to hear the branches reacting when we both trampled through them. Distance did not exist any longer and with it, the fear of being alone or of getting lost in the jungle also disappeared. Then the pain went away.

I started to smell the jungle, to discern the different shades of green, and observed the curious crawling animals that scurried off at every step I took. I perceived eyes that were watching me from every corner of the jungle, as if they were only one eye. Curious eyes. Silent eyes. Observing me as I walked. Creeping plants at my feet and stretching their tendrils upwards like long necks striving to catch a beam of sunlight. Shapes that were so different, unique, so alive in magical breathing. Something white flowed upwards along their stalks, something green flowed downwards like a body with veins. I felt the jungle was alive. The dry, fallen tree trunk was alive too. All life forms observed me with indescribable indifference.

The wind blew over the tree tops. Timid rays of sunlight filtered down through the thick foliage to kiss the ground. In response, the soil gently released whiffs of vapor that found their way into my lungs. I became damp jungle, water, soil, plant, wind, and sun.

Cuatiendioy wasn't nearby. He was only a ghost, a shadow vanishing in the distance, amongst the bulky, rough trunks of ancient trees. A shadow pursued by my shadow, moving as deftly as a ghost, empty, bodiless, only a spirit. We were the dry leaf, the *liana*, the bird and the insect, the fallen tree trunk, and the jaguar. We had one and the same rhythm. There was a perfect law. Nothing was destroyed. Everything was life at its fullest. Everything was transformation.

I don't know in what moment I caught up with Cuatiendioy. Walking side by side with him, I understood that this was what he was inviting me to do: *to become one with the jungle.* I felt the joy of being part of this marvelous experience. I wished the journey would never end. I knew that, in this state, I would be able to walk the rest of the afternoon and all night long. I started threading thoughts together, reflecting on the reason for this journey and lost control over my movements. Then I heard strange noises coming towards us. I thought it might be *indios.* I thought I heard the voices of children who were walking towards us. I could feel them getting closer. They spoke to each other in a strange language, with metallic sounds, and an intensity that grew progressively stronger until it created a kind of vibration that threw me severely off balance when it reached my ears.

Cuatiendioy made a forty-five degree turn without losing his rhythm and the throng felt closer. The foliage shifted and I turned to see what was causing the movement. I saw it was an army of ants. They were large and marching in order. Showing respect, Cuatiendioy avoided treading on them. I kept watching them for a while. I was puzzled that they could make so much noise. Then I lost my rhythm. I stumbled and fell down.

I tried to get up but couldn't. I felt my feet were worn out. I was certain I must have walked hundreds of kilometers. The ants no longer seemed so large to me. I didn't hear their noises either. The jungle was now the same as before: damp and cold.

Cuatiendioy stopped walking and said, "Too bad. At least, you've learned something."

I was glad to hear his words. I thought that I had finally managed to please him.

But then he continued, "You've learned not to be distracted. Always keep your rhythm. Don't get distracted. Remember this is not the *civilized man's* world. Here, you need to stop thinking and to feel the spirit of the jungle. We'll look for a place that will accept us."

"Right here. This place seems fine to me," I said because I had no wish to keep moving.

"How can you say that?" he replied. "How can you believe this place will accept us when you stumbled and fell down here? And even worse, when it doesn't even accept your footsteps, your tread, your way of living? No, Timoté. Nature makes you pay for everything."

"And what would it be making me pay for? All I did was to stumble over the trunk of a fallen tree. It can happen to anyone."

"Yes. To anyone who has as many debts to pay as you do."

"I don't have any debts," I insisted.

"No, this was only a message from the ants. I hope you have no other unpaid debts. Didn't you hear me? They are also a single spirit. Together they are only one, and even if you see them separate from one another, they are all only one, like the spirit of the water or of the wind. In that spirit also there is no distance or time. For the spirit, there is neither time or space. It is all one.

Become one with it! When they met you, they felt that, in some other place, you had killed them."

"Of course I have. I've killed tons of ants! But not here!"

"And who told you that there is a *here*? The *here* is only one. Whatever is happening *here,* is being felt *there.*"

"How come! What do you mean?"

"Nothing, Timoté. Let's go look for a place that will accept us."

I refused to keep going but Cuatiendioy insisted, "We need to continue. You wait right here for me. I'm going to look for a place that will accept us."

"I'm not getting up from here!" I shouted again.

He left for a few minutes and when he came back he said, "It's not possible for us to stay here. This area belongs to the ants. Their spirit says that you are not accepted, that they will give you no respite. It's better for us to leave."

"These are crazy notions of yours," I replied. "What kind of man talks with ants? You're crazy, Cuatiendioy."

"A *civilized man* doesn't talk with ants. I know that. He doesn't talk with butterflies either. Or with birds or flowers. He doesn't talk with the rivers, the forests, or the jungle. A *civilized man* only talks to himself. A *civilized man* is very scared of understanding life. That's why he fills himself with things and noises from the outside world. A *civilized man*, Timoté, cannot remain silent because silence exposes him. It leads him to his place of emptiness. And then what would happen with the mind that measures, compares, possesses and destroys?"

"And what could a man do without a mind, Cuatiendioy? It's what makes us different from all the other animals."

"It's true, Timoté. The *civilized man* lives entangled with everything he looks at. He will be more fully a man when he learns to direct his mind, to make it become still, to put it at *his* service, instead of him being at *its* service. A mind without direction is dangerous. The *civilized man* will need to return to *feeling* again. He needs to feel he is also ant, water, wind, and butterfly. But get up before the ants eat you alive."

I looked all over my body and saw tiny ants crawling on different parts of me; they were starting to sting me. I got up immediately and darted off after Cuatiendioy. When I caught up with him, he said, "We'll stop when we get to an area of palm trees."

We reached that place after walking for a long time. I dropped my body on the ground and fell fast asleep. When it got dark, and while I was half-sleep, I barely noticed how Cuatiendioy set up the *cambuche* and warmed up the *temascal*.

When I woke up, I felt highly sensitive. Maybe because of my diet of leaves, flowers, fruit, roots, colored water, coconuts and seeds. I didn't know what day it was or how much time had gone by. Cuatiendioy had the power of mixing everything up for me. He could make me feel cold in the sun and hot when it was cold. He would say, "Control, Timoté. Always stay in control."

Reflecting again about why I was there, I began to remember the second time I came across Cuatiendioy. It had been in circumstances that were similar to those of our first encounter.

It was a hot day in a town in the Northeast of the country, near the Pacific Ocean. I was walking, in a hurry. I was thirsty. Rumblings of battles could be heard in the distance. The cruel clashes between guerrilla fighters and the army were drawing near. That was why I was rushing along the street. Suddenly a strange force made me stop. It was as if an invisible mass was blocking my path, making it impossible for me to move forward. I was scared and looked anxiously in all directions. At one point, I fixed my gaze on a man who was coming up to me on the sidewalk. It was none other than Cuatiendioy. I recognized him as the indio with whom I had shared a glass of carambolo juice in that far off village.

"Don't run so fast, my friend. Sit down with me and let's have a beer together. Let the fear do the running. Send it away and let's enjoy this encounter."

His calm, soothing voice, the warm-hearted look in his eyes and the peacefulness of his words enabled me to feel confident enough to stop and enjoy the beer he was offering.

I quickly drank down the beer and, as I was in a hurry, I said, "Where do you live, my friend? I want to invite you to my house."

"Sure. One of these days," he replied. He went to return the empty bottle and stayed inside. I concluded he was having a conversation with someone, maybe a patient who needed to consult with him. I left. The clashes were now taking place near the town. The guerrillas were conquering more territory every day. Any man, whether humble or peasant, was useful to defend their cause or to serve either side as cannon fodder. I was never able to understand their cause. To me, they were the same as the military. They did the same thing. They killed!

I quickly went back home. I was scared. I had passed through villages that still smelled of gun powder and blood. I felt this was an utterly senseless war. It only left a trail of pain, widows, orphans, sadness and despair. That very same day, I gathered my few belongings and left that town on the first bus I could get.

I wanted to find a larger city, where I could blend in unnoticed and so be able to finish high school, far away from my parents and brothers. I was still a fugitive. I preferred to die while running away than killing or being killed in an absurd war.

Several days went by. I was working in a car repair shop, and moved about stealthily, taking all sorts or precautions.

One Saturday morning, someone knocked at my door. It was the indio, Cuatiendioy.

"Hello, my friend!" he said. He greeted me cordially, shaking my hand.

I was delighted to see him, and asked him in. We talked about trivial topics. I just saw him as an indio who sold herbs.

He didn't give me time to ask myself how he had found my house. Under his gaze, I felt out of control. He had arrived without having my address. It was a small city but still a city.

I hadn't recalled our third encounter until that day in the jungle, while I watched Cuatiendioy heating up a bit of wax over some green leaves over the fire. I asked him, "How did you manage to find my house that first time you came?"

Smiling, he said, "the *indio* knows, Timoté."

Then he went on to say, "Come, take a look at this. We are running out of *jimeritas* honey. We need to find their secret trove. It's a shame to rob them of it, but you know, we need to negotiate in order to live. This is a covenant. I have mine. What will yours be...?"

"I don't know anything about covenants with insects," I said.

"If you want to live here, in the jungle, and to obtain *jimeritas* honey, you'll have to make a covenant. Say it out loud or just in your mind. It's the same, provided you keep your promises. You need to understand that you are under the law of the jungle and of the *indio*."

I then thought I would defend and protect the jimeritas.

"Be very careful with your covenant, Timoté. Nature makes us pay for everything."

After this experience, I became very curious about these tiny insects. Later, I would devote several years to studying them, caring for them and keeping them with a view to preventing their extinction. I would try to obtain support from governmental agencies, and from a Non-Govermental Organization (NGO) but they argued that they had no resources for that kind of research.

But at that time, while I was making my covenant, Cutatiendioy observed me as if he were reading my mind, or seeing my future, and he said, "Poor Timoté. When have governments ever cared about preventive medicines found in Nature, or about protecting the resources of the *indios*? You'll have to defend them yourself. Show governments a deadly weapon and you'll become a millionaire. Don't talk to them about defending life because they'll think you're crazy. Observe, Timoté. The secret is in observing."

He heated the wax over the fire, and instantly, the air around us was pervaded by a sweet fragrance of wax or of flower lotion. Right then, several bees appeared.

"Do they sting?" I asked.

"These don't. The *jimeritas* will be arriving soon."

Just then, the mosquito-like insects appeared. They were so tiny that a normal bee was fifty times larger than they were. They were bees. Today, many years later, I can say they were Trigona bees, but at that time, I had no idea.

"They're here!" he exclaimed. They don't tell you where they live. We need to follow them." He took out a small bottle of blue ink from his bag. As he colored the honey with it, he smiled and remarked, "Watch how they get stained while they are sucking up the honey."

Sure enough, their tiny legs and wings were covered with honey. Even when they helped each other to clean it off, the color remained.

"So, what now?"

"Spread the honey around, hide the bottle, and let's wait. We're going to check the time it takes them to get back. This will tell us the distance. Watch the direction they're flying. They're going that way." He pointed with his finger. "Fine, we'll wait a bit now."

After a while, the painted ones came back, and many others as well. Cuatiendioy said, "They're about thirty meters away. Let's get going."

I followed him slowly, step by step, as in a walking meditation. His footsteps were imperceptible and he was in deep silence. We repeated the procedure of heating up the wax two or three times. The painted bees kept coming back more quickly each time.

Finally, I noticed that Cuatiendioy was looking closely at a dry branch hanging from a leafy tree. In a small hollow, we found the beautiful hive of these marvelous insects. Cuatiendioy drew near to it and moved his hands in circles over the fragile colony of tiny bees. They were really small, not more than two millimeters in size.

He took out his knife and delicately cut into the tree's bark, as if he were performing plastic surgery. This exposed to our view a number of tiny black bags, made of a very fragile type of wax. Even though his movements were slow, a large number of bees appeared and surrounded the tiny bags.

"In any case, one has to ask for permission, Timoté. This queen doesn't like to share her trove and just because they are defenseless doesn't mean that we're going to take advantage of them. Watch, Timoté. This is one of the few places on earth where several queens can live together in the same house. Only one of them is a mother. The rest are virgins. That means they wait patiently or wisely either for their mother to die or for the population of the hive to grow large enough to split and form a new kingdom. Only one of them will become a queen. The others will only be queens over themselves. They will die crownless. That is, without ever having copulated with a drone. See how wonderful it is? There is an order in everything. If you could see this, you would realize that it's an organized and well planned world. It's almost perfect. If we humans could learn to live like this, the earth would be totally different.

He pulled out a small bamboo tube from his backpack. From the tube, he took out a tiny sharp hook, made from a bird's claw. He used it to cut the layer of wax that covered the honey. His cuts were as delicate as a surgeon's. As a result, some tiny black bags made of a fragile wax material came into view. He made an extremely small puncture on the back of each of them, thus exposing the precious liquid.

"We must be careful not to disturb the peace of this humble abode excessively," Cuatiendioy continued. "We'll wait until the queen comes out. You'll see."

After a few minutes, a large bee appeared. It was very different from all the others. It had a bulky belly, covered in attractive stripes. It was luminous and beautiful, like all Queens are. She went about nervously, checking the cells that covered the tiny eggs, and also inspecting the offspring that were in their own cells, waiting for the moment of their maturity to arrive so they could come out. All this time, an army of guardian bees escorted her, flying in circles around her.

"That one's the queen. It has come out to check out the disturbance we are causing. Just watch her with no thought in your mind other than becoming one with her. Remember we are all one same energy, one same thing. We are all one. Think about your covenant. As you know, I already have mine."

"I can't make my mind quiet, I can't help admiring such beauty but I don't know how to communicate with insects."

"Drop the noise. Set your eyes and your heart on the colony. Breathe at its rhythm. Don't contaminate what you feel."

The colony had been opened up, exposed. Nervously, the bees were trying to repair the little bags Cuatiendioy had cut open with his small hook.

Cuatiendioy had his gaze fixed on the center of the colony. His impressive silence inspired a feeling of peace in me. I had no choice but to try to imitate him, although for me, the priority was the trove. With only very few movements, I could extract the wax bags with their delicious contents.

However, I knew I had to wait for Cuatiendioy. He had a different way of viewing nature. I gave up. I realized that he was not going to extract the honey until I became silent. In other words, until I started imitating him.

I set my gaze on the colony again and began to control my breathing. I merged with the colony's rhythm again. At one point, a tingling sensation spread all over my body, as if all the bees were walking on my skin and at the same time as if they were covering up all the space around us. Slowly, the little bees drew away from the honey bags, leaving us free space for our extraction task.

At that moment, Cuatiendioy reached in again to extract the honey bags, moving with caution so as to avoid damaging the cells of the offspring. He handed me a little, dark-brown wax bag, with such a thin covering that it burst open at the slightest contact with my fingers, releasing a sweet and delicious trickle of this elixir of the jungle. He waited patiently while I chewed on the wax bag. It felt like a wad of sticky chewing gum when it clings to teeth.

Then he took out a small amber colored bottle from his backpack. He removed its cap and delicately extracted the honey from the bags until the bottle was full.

I was expecting him to take all of the bags in the colony, but he just filled up his bottle and began to close up the colony using the same wax he had previously removed. He did this as carefully as when he had cut it open. He bowed to the colony, and said, "Don't forget your covenant. We need to move on, but don't forget your aim. Have you seen something yet?"

"Like what?"

"Well, that's not important. What matters is that with this precious nourishment, our bodies will live, healthy and grateful. This moment is unique and unrepeatable. There will never be a day like this one again. In order to remember it clearly, you will have to come back to the experience. When you learn to live without measuring time, every moment will be eternal. Meanwhile, we'll get some rest and we'll continue with your healing."

"Sit down here," he instructed. "Straighten up your backbone. Don't close your eyes. Keep your gaze straight ahead and your eyes unfocused. Your past can be today. Just bring your mind to stillness and let yourself be carried away."

He touched my spine again, and asked me, "What do you see, Timoté?"

"I've convinced my father not to send me away to a school in the city. I'll be attending a rural school. I'm negotiating with my father. I'll have to walk five kilometers to get to school. That will be ten, with the walk back home.

"I'm so happy! Dad is worried. On my first day of class, he has given me a squirrel, to be my pet. It lives with me, in my shirt pocket.

"Mom doesn't want me to take it to school. I'm crying. I'm convincing her with my tears. I use my tears as a weapon. She allowed me to do this

when I was even younger. Mom is talking to the school principal. The principal is admitting me to the school, with a few conditions. I'm already in the classroom, with Toto. That's how I named my pet squirrel. All the kids are very fond of him. Toto plays with everyone. I'm so happy! Seeing my pet fitting into the school, and seeing that he becomes the center of attention for all my classmates. They all want to feed him crumbs from their snacks.

"From the beautiful school yard, I am contemplating Mount Viringo. It is a tall and beautiful mountain. The rivers that flow through my father's farm have their source up there. The days go by. I go up and down everywhere, treading on the mud, through the dust and the meadows. There is new magic in every day. I can feel how everything changes in an instant. Even my body. A changing mass that stays behind on the road.

"There's a different atmosphere in the school today. A strange uneasiness. I don't know how to describe the feeling. The flowers are alive. This much the teacher has taught me. And he has spoken to me about the importance of looking after them and watering them. I've done that. I've watered them so many times at home but I had never seen them so beautiful and so sad.

"I don't know what's happening or what's going to happen. I'm feeling something in my legs. I'm walking home. It's not weariness from too much walking. I know because it's what I do every day. I'm resting under an avocado tree. Toto is climbing up in search of something to eat. I'm waiting for him. I've often waited for him on that spot, while he searches for his favorite fruit. There is always a pleasant silence in this spot. But it's different today. I'm uneasy. The forest is uneasy. It's the same uneasiness I have sometimes felt when something sad happens. Something startles me. A rifle shot! Over there! Toto has dropped dead at my feet! He's dead! No! It's not possible!"

"Come back". "You're crying".

"Someone has killed my pet. I remember. I loved him so much, and a hunter killed him. It was very, very sad, for me and for all the children in the school."

"Maybe you could have listened to the warning from the flowers?" Cuatiendioy said. "They were sad. You said so yourself. You also felt the uneasiness of the forest and even so, you could do nothing because life has an inexplicable rhythm in the *civilized man's* mind."

"What do you mean by that?"

"Nothing. Nothing yet. Nothing you can't discover on your own. You can do it. It's true. You will live like a *civilized man*, feeling nothing. And even when you do feel, you'll deny what you feel. And even when you do see, you'll deny that you see. Such has been your education.

"They have restrained everything in you. They have restrained your capacity to feel. Everything will be restrained *until you become one with everything*.

"So you saw that the flowers were sad? Why didn't you enquire into the sadness of the flowers? And if your legs felt heavy, why didn't you ask them questions? Nature sends out all the messages much before events take place. If you had stopped to listen to the warnings from nature, maybe you wouldn't have lost your pet. Listen and feel those messages from the places where you live. If you don't learn to do that, then beware of the jungle. First you have to walk with your spirit, in order to feel the jungle until you no longer have a *civilized man's* mind. You need to be the mind of everything. Just as I've always told you. Become one with everything because you are everywhere and you are nowhere. Then, you know nothing, Timoté.

"But it's all right. You paid for not having seen and for not having listened. That is, for being caught up in the noise you've always lived in. Free yourself from the pain today. You implanted it into your flesh when you started hating the hunter. Look the hunter in the eye. Forgive him and straighten up your backbone. You need to understand there is a hatred that is as deadly as the bullet that killed your pet. Why do you think they are all killing each other out there? And what do you see all around? Hatred.

Hatred attracts hatred, just as blood attracts blood. And people's cancers spread all around, collecting the debts that are owed to them. This savagery never ends. And don't even think of the cities. The horror would kill you."

"Yes, Cuatiendioy. But how can I find the hunter again? I don't even know if he's still alive."

"It doesn't matter whether he's alive or not out there. What I see is that he's still alive in you. At least in the hatred you have embedded into your flesh. Every pain has an origin but hatred is the deadliest. Hatred kills, Timoté. It kills the one who carries it within. It's a burden as heavy as fear. Fear kills. Envy also kills.

"Reflect about the pains in your back. Now that we're touching upon interesting issues, I want you to remain in the same place where you were born. Look closely at the burden you've taken upon your shoulders so that you can straighten up your backbone more, and we can mover forward in your search."

I had barely begun to recover from the trance he had put me in when, in a flash, he touched my backbone again and took me back to the past.

"What do you see?"

"I'm at home. Dad's in the stable, milking the cows. I'm drinking a cup of warm milk. It's delicious. A truck is approaching the stable. My father has sold several cows. They don't want to climb on to the truck. They're being beaten with a whip. Oh! They're crying. Dad is suffering at the sight of the cows' suffering. One cow licks my father's hand. The cow is crying. So is my father. I don't want to see any more. Please. No!"

"All right, come back,"

"I can easily remember the scenes, Cuatiendioy. It seems like only yesterday. I can feel the resistance in some of the cows, the silence in the meadows, some grey clouds cast over the morning. I can hear the anguish of the bull, saying good bye to his partners. I see the corral as a death trap and I'm sorry for the departure of the cows, who fed me when I was a young child. I feel ungrateful and I feel I'm guilty of complicity in sending them off on this journey from which they will not return. I see them as a part of my family. The men who are taking them away only see them as meat. They're heartless businessmen. Since then, my father made the decision to never again sell any of his cows. He kept them on the meadows until they died of old age."

"You see? It's only a cow," Cuatiendioy said. "Your father was able to experience feeling for the cow, and you don't know what price he had to pay for that. Do you want to know?"

"No, please. Of course not," I replied.

"That's what man is like. He has a cow, that is noble and humble. It provides him with milk, cheese and calves. And when he no longer has any use for it, he kills it and eats it, without giving it the slightest chance to defend itself. He does the same with chickens, horses, and other beings. A man strokes a little piglet and makes it think he's fond of it, and then he kills it and eats it. That's what man is like, Timoté. Let's continue, then. Only now I don't know where to take you so you can see or feel. But of one thing I'm sure: if you saw everything there is in the city, the horror would kill you. It will be better to keep looking inside because in the outside world everything is depressing and hard to accept."

"I'm very scared, Cuatiendioy. I think I don't want to continue remembering my past. How else can I keep my mind busy?"

"Not here, Timoté. As you can see, you haven't got much to entertain your mind here except the jungle itself and you haven't become one with it yet. You don't feel concerned about any of this because you're convinced that your own issues are what matters. Crouch down on the ground and listen to the calls of the earth. Press your ears to the ground like I do, and listen to the larger heart of everything that exists. Can you hear something, Timoté? Can you hear something?"

"I only hear the birds singing and the sound of the wind among the branches."

"No. Listen to the call of the jungle. The *ceibas* are falling. I can hear them hitting the ground. Let's pray for the earth."

"Pray! What do you mean 'pray'? You've never said a prayer. I didn't know you prayed."

"The *indio* prays, the *indio* feels. He prays to Mother Nature and asks forgiveness for the *civilized man*'s ignorance. He prays to the sun and gives thanks for its infinite power to give life. He prays to the water. He prays to the rain. He prays to the wind. He prays to the God who touches the seeds and turns them into plants. He prays to that spirit that gives the deer its movement, and to the spirit of the *yuko (a juicy fruit)*. The *indio* knows that if he gives offence, the *indio* is punishing himself.

"The *civilized man* doesn't understand anything. He prays to an unknown God and kills life. He understands nothing. He has understood nothing. As you saw, there was a felling of *ceibas*. The jungle does not forgive and the earth will not forgive. As long as the black spaces are not repaired, the energy of the earth won't circulate as it should and it will cause changes that we will all regret. By then you will have learned how to manage anguish and how to cure the soul. The *civilized man* needs to know where his misfortunes come from."

He walked up to a tree that was still standing but dying. He embraced it and said: "Oh, brother spirit of the jungle. You who live so simply and offer yourself so simply so that everything can move forward. You are firm in everything. Even in death."

We picked up our backpacks and walked away from that beautiful place, carrying with us the wonderful treasure that is the *jimerita* honey.

I used to believe that the honey of these marvelous insects existed only in the Amazon but I tasted it again in Honduras and in the south of Mexico. By then, there were few bees left, due to the falling of forests and the fires. As some species of *meliponineo (stingless bee)* were confused with Africanized bees [*Apis melifera adansonii*], their colonies were destroyed and burned.

IV

Healing The Past

We moved forward in a state of fulfillment and harmony. I didn't know whether it was due to the properties of the *jimerita* honey or the result of all the healing of the soul, as Cuatiendioy called it.

We arrived at a beautiful place, a clear area with tall vegetation surrounded by pastureland where the most exotic animals of the jungle were resting very peacefully; Some of them could only be seen around the natural arbor of the trees like the red-bellied titi, or the golden-bellied tamarin, both of the family of monkeys. They were lying on their backs sunbathing without any concern about the feared jaguar hanging around the area, who also showed no concern about the *capybara* or *agouti*—his favorite prey, that were roaming around. The jaguar did not even care about us either; this place belonged to everybody where the sun was giving warmth to all of us without any preference. This clear space amidst the thick and dense jungle seemed like an eye peeking to the heavens that allowed us to watch the naked firmament.

Cuatiendoy bowed his head to all the animals as if greeting them or asking for permission to start the bonfire; this feared threat of the fire that drove away all visitors became our best ally and protection.

We started the bonfire before total darkness settled in. We sat down as usual in silence and entered that state where only communication without words exists. Using the language of the soul, we both were embraced by the Void. The firmament was clearly seen with a breathtaking beauty; I could see distant stars and began fantasizing that they were inhabited by other beings. The stars were my companion and I thought that maybe Cuatiendoy knew something about them that I was not aware of.

When I focused my attention on Cuatiendoy there was something strange happening between us. There was a feeling I had never perceived before, and which caused a bit of uneasiness. I came close to Cuatiendioy. I could see there was deep sadness in his eyes for the first time. I sat beside him and we remained in silence for a while. After that, when the flames began to shed light on our space, he asked me to keep the eyes open without getting distracted. He then instructed me on how to follow him and we danced to the rhythm of *"hueeeejahueeeejahiona... hueeeejahueeeejahiona...huejahionaaaa hay hayhay..."*

We repeated the song so many times that even up to this day, it comes back to me in my dreams. I never knew the meaning of that word, *"huejahiona,"* because it no longer mattered. What mattered was what I felt and what I saw.

Cuatiendioy and I enjoyed this, and he said, "You can also sing like this to life, to the flowers and to the earth. What's the point of singing to women so much if we don't first sing to our Mother Earth?

In that moment, I remembered I had a girlfriend. I hadn't seen her in a long time. I asked Cuatiendioy, "What day is it today?"

"Which today!" he replied. "It's nighttime. Why don't you gaze at a star?"

"What's the date today, Cuatiendioy?"

"It's this date."

"And, what's that?"

"I don't know. That's something which is important only for *white men*. Observe the moon and work it out."

"How?"

"Oh, Timoté! The *civilized man* worries about time because everything has restrictions for him. Even life. He looks into a mirror and compares himself from day to day and from year to year. And that's why his life is shortened. If the years don't make him grow old, the mirror does. The mirror shortens the number of years you're going to live because you compare and measure the unfolding of your life in it. And this leads you to accept that life must be like the reflection in the mirror. *White men* are fools, Timoté. They seek for a reflection in everything, in order to be accepted, to be loved, or to be important. The reflection becomes more important than the one the mirror shows us. That's why the *indio* doesn't like mirrors. And he doesn't like photographs either, because they are both objects that rob you of your spirit. The *indio* worries when he doesn't feel. When the jungle conceals its mysteries from him. When the plants conceal their power. Or when the *civilized man* comes along to create mirrors for him and to restrict his spirit. We don't like the *civilized man's* life and we don't like his death either. Their lives are full of fears because their gods are very far way from them, and their gods punish them when they die. That's why white folks are afraid of life and of death. We *indios* have our gods closer to us. No further away than our eyes. For us, dying is a moment of resting because the *indio* never dies. He continues living in the magic of the jungle."

I felt uneasy and no matter how hard I tried to calm down, I couldn't. I found it even harder to conceal my anxiety. Something was robbing me of my peacefulness. After touching my head for a long while, and feeling Cuatiendioy's relentless gaze on me, I heard him ask, "What are you worried about?"

"My girlfriend."

"And what do you feel?

"I feel sorry for her because she's not here with me..."

"Say what you feel, Timoté. You don't need to hide anything here. Maybe I can help you. You live entangled in your important things. I mean, you live entangled in your thoughts, with everything you have done with your reality, your '*important*' reality. Well, then. Whatever it is, I'll try to help you. Only your concern is not about anything in the jungle. We've spent enough time together to know you're not upset by something in your immediate surroundings. What's bothering you is something else. Release that feeling, Timoté."

I took out my note book and wrote down my feelings. Then I read them aloud to him while he listened attentively, as if it were the most important thing in his life.

> *My poor absent girlfriend,*
> *with such a wealth of pain.*
> *Who says I am only fond of her,*
> *when I simply love her?*
> *If she looks for me, she can't find me.*
> *If she finds me, I'm not there.*
> *Why do you look for me in distant places*
> *when we are so near to each other?*
> *My poor absent girlfriend.*
> *She believes I'm only fond of her*
> *and I simply love her.*

"I like that poem, Timoté. I think it contains feeling. She's thinking of you right now. All you need to do is send it to her."

"But, how? Who would help me deliver it to her?"

We went over to the bonfire and while we danced around the flames, Cuatiendioy would repeat with me:

> *My poor absent girlfriend*
> *With such a wealth of pain*
> *She believes I'm truly fond of her*
> *And I am simply in love with her.*

That night I slept with my girlfriend in my arms.

Cuatiendioy said, "You need to love until you sweat love. And you need to love every single drop of sweat. The depth of your life depends on how intensely you live each moment. Only the moment matters. Breathe it in deeply, Timoté."

The next day, I felt sad. I didn't know how long I'd been away. I wondered whether my girlfriend would still be waiting for me to return, after having left her alone for such a long time. I also wondered if there might be some other cause for my sadness.

Cuatiendioy was looking at me closely. He said: "An emotion, Timoté. You need to find its source. An emotion has no age. It lives in a timeless present and prevents you from seeing and connecting with true feeling. Bad emotions are the enemies of *white men.*

"A bad emotion is an evil spirit. If it came to you when you were two years old, it will always be two years old. Even if you live to be a hundred, it will be two years old. That's why you need to find the signs of what produced it. They get embedded in your flesh, Timoté. They're painful because they get into your body. They are the cause of the illnesses of the *civilized man*.

"But man must change. He's been lost for too long. He needs to accept that he's lost. Searching for the meaning of life, he filled himself with things, without respecting the life of the earth.

"Some day, *white men* will change, and they'll come to see all of this differently. One day they will become one with the earth. But they must do it before the last *ceiba* in the jungle dies. The *civilized man* must abandon his wise man's pride. He must stop looking upwards so much and first start defending what we have down here, instead. I've always lived in the mountains and have experienced how one can hear the sounds of the streams less and less. And the same happens with the sounds of the rivers and the trees. I've seen the birds leave and disappear forever before my very eyes. I have seen *white men* praying to God, asking Him to grant that the bullet with which they wish to kill their enemy will not fail. I have felt the waves of hatred in the *white men's* protests. I have seen very little love. *White men* have hung up *indios* from the trees just for eating one of their cows. They have invaded our land, they have caused our crops to wither and ravaged our fields, contaminated our rivers, despised and desecrated the indio's wisdom. Love, Timoté, seek for its space. You need to allow that love to spread from you, through you, and to express itself without fear. It's the only thing that will make you free from the rifle, from fear, and from war.

"Love is what can give you the courage to live. To experience yourself free from attachments. Because it encompasses everything, and carries no burden except the joy of existence. There are no limits, borders, nor languages you cannot understand. There are no worlds it does not overrun, just as there are no jungles it does not walk through. It's the first step in your search of a meaning for life. And here, the *indio* loves the jungle. It's the only real thing we possess. He feels its vibrations. He loves the Earth. It is perhaps the only love he recognizes and the only thing he belongs to, after his tribe. You'll see that here you will lose your fear of living. Living in the simplicity of feeling. Loving pure and simple, and letting your feeling burst out into the open air. Love puts a special brightness in the eyes of those who love. It carries the sound of a cricket, leisurely and harmonious, and the light of fireflies clustered in the night sky. Love everything, Timoté. Become one with everything—with what you see and feel. Become sound. Become forest. Love the silence that transports you to worlds without borders."

After that, Cuatiendioy remained silent. I was left expectant, overwhelmed by everything I was hearing from an *indio* who seemed to be a wise man, speaking about love. Then he went on to say, "You can say that you love but don't confuse it with desire. It doesn't matter if you don't know what it is. What matters is that you should be open to receive it."

By then, I was no longer hearing him. He was touching my soul. I felt a bit scared.

He just kept on contemplating our small bonfire. He sensed my fear, and said, "Timoté, a man's most dangerous enemy is, and will always be, fear. Discover it! The weapons are in your body. Sit down every day, as firm as an oak, as motionless as a rock, letting your thoughts roam as free as the wind, clinging to nothing until you find peace. The peace *white men* have lost and no longer know how to find. And it's no further away than the same place where they've lost it.

"If you find peace, there will no longer be any fear. But if fear prevents you from reaching your peace, always keep looking in front of you, never to the left because this will only make your fear grow stronger. If it still persists, look upwards. Advancing is always upwards because that's where you create your present. In order to be in the void, look in front of you. Look to your right and upwards if you need something. If you lose your balance, soften your gaze. Remember, you will need to discover and confront your sadness. For this, Timoté, you don't need to do anything. Blessed be the man who is capable of sitting down and doing nothing."

"Is that what you do every evening, Cuatiendioy? Is that why you remain sitting for such a long time, seeming as if you were out of touch with reality?"

"That's right. I like nothingness. But we'll talk about that some other time. We can talk about nothingness only after you've made contact with it yourself. For now, we'll continue with your process. You need to clean out every feeling that is upsetting you. We need you to become healthier day by day, so we can travel together through the jungle. You need to bear in mind that everything that happens to us happens for a reason, and that there is something to learn in everything. If you understand this, then you will know why you came to the jungle. And why you came to earth. You will not be afraid because fear comes from not knowing. Do you understand why you don't know this? Because you are afraid to bring your mind to a stop. Or you can't. Or you don't want to because you are afraid of knowing. Afraid of knowing that you can see beyond what you always look at, that you can see we are not what we think we are, that you look at everything like the *civilized man* looks at it.

"Begin by silencing the noise in your mind. Follow the sound of the jungle. Become one with it before it forces you to. You need to become united to it, or it will devour you without mercy. Listen to the messengers of the jungle. Look for an ally. Measure every step in your feeling. Forget about suffering. What you learned from the *civilized man* is worthless here. The sadness you bring with you affects you because with it, you are always measuring and comparing everything. You go back to memories, and feeling bad brings you comfort. But this is the jungle. And you need to know what you came here for."

Touching my spine again, he asked, "What do you see now, Timoté?"

"*I'm at home. It's a rainy afternoon. I feel the raindrops as if they were tears. My father's arms are listless and his heart does not beat as it always does. He seems sad. It's a different sadness from the one we feel when my brothers go away after a visit. My cousin is leaving tomorrow. He's the one who helps my father with the horses and the cattle. My cousin is a sad young man. He frequently leaves and then comes back during harvest times.*

"*My father wants to persuade him to stay. He offers to raise his salary. But he has already packed his battered leather suitcase, the one he has always used in his numerous travels. He rejects the offer. He also sits down to contemplate the afternoon. His silence is a sad one. It's as if he were carrying something immense within his suitcase. A deep sorrow. There is a sadness pervading thoughout our house while the night sleeps.*

"*It's the next day, now. The cocks sing their welcome to the morning. My father saddles the horses and fastens the suitcase. My cousin says goodbye to all of the things he sees. He's leaving but he doesn't look at me. I seek out his shifty, uneasy eyes. He's saying goodbye to me now. He strokes my head. His hands are cold. My mother bids him farewell with her prayers and her tears. My cousin has said goodbye to everything. He rides away along the trail. There is a strange silence. The striped cuckoo is singing on the guarumo tree. Country folks say it's a bird of ill omen. There is a black butterfly in the room that used to be my cousin's. My mother chases it away. She says it does not bring anything good. It's a long day, full of uneasiness.*

"*With nightfall, darkness has come. The horses are very restless. I can hear there is someone in the stable. He's walking about and cutting up fodder. 'Maybe our cousin is back,' my mother says. It's a dark and unquiet night.*

With my father and my cousin away, we feel lonely and can't sleep.

"*The following day starts with a stranger at our door. He's very upset because he brings terrible news. Our cousin is dead. He's committed suicide. I don't want to see any more, Cuatiendioy. Please, get me out of here!"*

"That's all for today", said Cuatiendioy.

I came back from that trance in a state of agitation. My past was as present as the feelings of anguish and frustration. I felt guilty for not having asked my cousin about his deep sadness.

"It was my fault, Cuatiendioy! How is it possible that I did nothing to save my cousin! How could I let him commit suicide! I knew about his sadness and his deep pain."

"There was nothing you could have done, even when you knew and even if the messengers had warned you. It was your cousin's decision. He had already made that decision and sooner or later, he would have killed himself. There's only one part of life the *civilized man* understands: the one that measures, the one he can grasp with his senses. But there's something beyond the senses, where any explanation is useless. There's something beyond the senses. Something the *civilized man* has lost."

"It was my first contact with death. I loved my cousin as an older brother. He was twenty-eight and he used to help me with my homework. His death was very painful for me."

"That's the way it is, Timoté. Sometimes it's better not to know too much so you can avoid suffering. Or it is better to understand where the suffering comes from, so that you can accept it. But of course, in true knowledge, there is no suffering. Suffering killed your cousin. He didn't know how to still his mind. Sometimes fear is brave. Suffering is the result of ignorance."

"I had never noticed that bird's song before. Countryside folks called it *tres pies* (three feet) because when it sings, it sounds as if it were chanting '*trespieeeés, trespieeeés.*' They believed it was an ill omen when its song was heard."

"It was a messenger, Timoté."

"What do you mean by *'a messenger'*?"

"Messengers exist, once you discover them. From then on, you can turn them into your allies. We *indios* have always had our allies. In order to have them, you need to respect nature. Not respecting it is altering it and when you alter it, you are harming yourself. The *civilized man* has sought alliances with the dog, the horse, the cow, the chickens and many other animals. He's forged alliances but he's never cared about understanding the ways in which the animals try to communicate with him. That's because he has looked down upon them, calling them inferior creatures. He hasn't taken the time to listen to them because he's full of his own noise about how to exploit them more efficiently. Never look down upon the so-called inferior creatures. They have a lot to teach us. You need to discover the messengers of the jungle yourself, and find your ally.

"At least, you know now that if the *tres piés* (striped cuckoo) sings, or if a black butterfly alights on your bed, you will die that very day. It would be better for you to have allies in the jungle, instead of being so afraid of military service. Ever since you escaped, you've been carrying the burden of that rifle on your shoulders."

I didn't find his comment at all funny. I was a fugitive. That was the reason why I was here in the jungle But I hadn't told anyone about this. I had been captured by the military. I had been in a cell for several days with neither water or food, and then forcibly enlisted and sent out into combat. This meant I was supposed to kill but my deepest feelings made this impossible for me. For all everyone knew, including my family, I had been killed in combat. But I had never told anyone that I was a fugitive.

But I felt I needed to give Cuatiendioy a prompt answer.

"I can't kill," I replied. I didn't dare ask him how he knew about this part of my life that I had kept a closely guarded secret. I felt uncomfortable and I wondered whether the version he had of my past was an accurate one. I decided to clear up the issue. So I told him the reason why I had accepted his invitation to go into the jungle was that I was looking for a safe place where the army would never find me. I also wanted to avoid going to that area on the Pacific, known as the Apartadó, where anyone who was in serious trouble with the law sought refuge. It was a place rife with prostitution, illegal trading, criminals and guerrilla fighters. It was also a place of great wealth forged on the exploitation of laborers of African ancestry, forced to work in mines and on farms where they were treated virtually as slaves.

Such was my distress at the possibility of finding myself carrying a rifle again that I begged him to keep my secret. He listened attentively. Under his penetrating eyes, I felt self-confident. He inspired in me the peacefulness I lost whenever any memory of the army came to my mind.

He let me speak for a long while. Then he sat down closer to me and without shifting his gaze away from me, he said, "Timoté, could you tell me your story again?"

I didn't understand. I had no doubt that he had been far more attentive than any of my friends and even my parents, would have been during such a long narrative. And now he was asking me to repeat it!

"I want you to tell me the story again, but this time put feeling into it. The excitement you felt when you escaped, and the fear you experienced with the rifle in your hand. Put feeling into it, Timoté."

I began to tell my story again, leaving out no details. He fixed his gaze on me, his black eyes, shiny and penetrating. He followed closely each and every one of my words. He plunged into my story like as if he were present in every one of its images. The feeling became pleasant. Everything I had seen and felt changed. My agitated heart changed its rhythm. The chill that those memories brought to my body was transformed into a pleasant and enjoyable warmth.

In his eyes, I could see the reflection of my second story. Or that my story lost itself in his eyes. I don't know what were behind them but I just couldn't introduce fear in my narrative when I spoke. I came to the end of the story of my past. I didn't know how long it had taken. I only knew it was over because Cuatiendioy closed his eyes and entered a state of silence.

As I tried to stand up, I realized how much time had gone by when I felt the stiffness in every cell of my body. I was in pain all over and I didn't know where to start to feel my legs. I didn't know how to summon my legs. They remained almost welded together. I couldn't bear the slightest physical contact. I forgot my body and the pain I was feeling due to my cross-legged posture. My past no longer mattered now. I had a deep feeling of peacefulness. There was no longer any fear in the memories from my past. What strange process had taken place by telling Cuatiendioy my story? What magic was there in his gaze? Where did his eyes take me, once he fixed them on mine? On those occasions, I was transported through a tunnel where only that moment existed, and nothing else could exist. I realized that when I went into my story, the present had vanished. My life had gone back in time, to such an extent that my stiffened and aching body was completely forgotten.

But then my attention was directed at finding the way to become free from that pain. I undertook the conquest of my body by means of gentle movements. Finally, I managed to stand up. Taking slow steps, I found a *guaje* and drank some water to soothe my throat. I had been speaking for so long that I was certain I wouldn't speak again for the rest of the day.

After that, I went for a walk in our immediate surroundings. I found the jungle had become interesting and beautiful to me. But confusing thoughts came to my mind, such as, if I'm not afraid of the army any more, what am I doing here?

As I gradually became connected with the present, new doubts appeared and other painful experiences from the past started coming back to my mind. I wondered about the future, and the present lost relevance. Fear began to take over my body again. I went back to our camp, looking for Cuatiendioy. I found him making some weird movements.

"Come closer, Timoté. These exercises will keep you in contact with your body. Learn how to center your energy and how to direct it to ease your pain."

"I don't have any pain. It's all gone. I'd rather have some rest now."

"Living through your past again was a very intense experience. There are many things you will need to change. I can see your whole life has been mapped out based on fear, and that you're addicted to it. It's hard to talk with *white men*. Very few of them are not addicted to fear. They find nourishment and pleasure in their fears. As you can see for yourself, it hasn't been two hours since I showed you how well one can live without fear. But you've connected with it again because you're an addict. You need your fear in order to live. You feel lost without it. It was fear that brought you here and you've turned to your past for refuge. You also fear the future. You live in a senseless present, with an uneasy mind, always striving to be recognized or loved, always looking outside for the cause of your unhappiness. A short while ago, all your concern was about fear of the army. You don't have that concern any more right now but you'll have it again, because that was the nourishment of your life, the reason for defending it, for running. You feel it's better to have your mind full of noise than to sit down to contemplate the jungle.

"All *white men* are afraid. Because of their fear, they destroy the earth. Because of their fear, they are wiping out the jungle. Because of their fear, they kill each other. They bring their fears with them and contaminate everything. They enjoy anything that makes them feel fear and they destroy whatever they can't understand. They're addicts, and you're an addict too. I can see that listening to me is making you feel fear. But that's all right. You'll have time to free yourself from it. As from tomorrow, you'll be on your own.

"In order to be able to confront your past, first you need to change what you have learned from the *civilized man*. It doesn't matter that you're one of them. Here, you'll cut yourself free a bit from their way of thinking. After all, it's very easy. You just need to change the story in your mind, forgiving your past and of course also paying the debts you owe the earth. She demands payment of all debts, Timoté. The earth is our mother. She will put an end to the ill treatment we inflict on her. No one will be spared from her without payment. The *indio* says that what the *civilized man* fears is the punishment the earth will inflict. She gives the *civilized man* everything but the *civilized man* wants more. He wants to save, to have treasures, because he's afraid of the future. And so he wastes his life. If he doesn't become one with the earth, but without trying to possess her, he will die in fear. What the earth has for the *civilized man* is the secret of peace, the secret of life, the mystery of death. She has everything. There is nothing other than her. Become one with her and you'll be able to become one with yourself. Tomorrow you will be on your own. Begin by feeling the wind, and then become wind. Don't let fear be the guide of your life. If you become one with the jungle, you will find allies that will make your stay easier. Don't get distracted with the past. It's gone. Now it's time for you to go on your own search for silence, and to find it yourself.

"If you follow my trail, you'll only become an *indio*. I don't want you to imitate me and become an *indio*. That would be the same as exchanging your fears for something else. You need to find yourself. You can rely on external allies to help you, but you need to find your own internal ally. And even though it may sound strange to you, it is only in true silence that you'll find all of your allies. They will help you to find clarity regarding your concerns. And one day, the allies will no longer be needed. You will become one with everything that exists. There will be no time, no past, no future. It's also time for me to visit my people. I'll be going home. No one will find you here."

"And where will I stay?"

"You'll stay right here. Do you feel this space is not large enough for you? With no noises, no bustle, no army or murderers?"

"I'm not staying here, Cuatiendioy. We came into the jungle together and we'll leave the jungle together."

"I'm not leaving the jungle," he replied. "I'll just be going home for a visit. You can't come with me without permission from Tandioy."

"And who's that?"

"He's the chief of my tribe. He has never accepted *white men*. But send him something of yours and see if he accepts you."

"Like what? I have nothing."

"What a fool you are! How can you think that Tandioy needs something from you for his own benefit? Tandioy is a *Curaca*. Whatever you have on you has become you. That's what Tandioy will see. And if he approves of you, we can go together on my next trip. Nothing bad will happen to you here. Become one with everything."

"And the jaguar?"

"The jaguar has been walking side by side with us all this time. Just as the snake, the eagle, the wild boar, the raccoon and the deer. You need to understand that if the jungle had wanted to, it would have devoured you already. There must be something good about you. Maybe your foolishness."

He went over to the *temascal* and checked the knots of the *lianas* that kept the branches fastened together. This one was the best of all the *temascales* he had built so far. It was also set up in a larger clearing than the previous ones. Those were clear indicators that he had planned it all carefully. There was no doubt in my mind that he was going to leave me on my own while he visited his family.

That evening we prepared the tea and performed our customary ritual of sipping it as we sat together by the campfire. There was a difference from previous evenings, however. On this occasion Cuatiendioy did not drink his tea in silence. Instead he kept talking to me. He gave me advice on how to keep my balance. And most importantly, how to face, when I was on my own, the most dangerous enemy of man: FEAR.

While he was giving me instructions, I was working out the way of following his tracks. After all, he had taught me how to follow tracks in the jungle and how to smell other bodies. After a while, he fell silent and took up his usual posture, sitting with his legs crossed, in the lotus position, and fixing his gaze in front of him with his eyes wide open. He seemed to see everything and at the same time, nothing

I couldn't sleep that night, thinking I would be alone and not knowing where I was. I felt panic. So I decided not to sleep at all and to keep watch over any movement Cuatiendioy might make.

But I was too worn out and finally, I did fall asleep.

V

Abandoned To Silence

When I woke up, I was alone. I realized Cuatiendioy had left. This made me feel both irritated and sad. That was exactly how Cuatiendioy had always been. He would show up suddenly, and then he would disappear just as suddenly. But I had never imagined the possibility that he would abandon me in the very heart of the Amazon jungle.

He left me a jar of *jimerita honey*, the flint stones to start the fire with, a knife, a *guaje,* and a large supply of *yuko.* Now I understood the reason why he had been giving me advice on how to deal with fear. Clearly all this time, he had been preparing me for this moment. I went out in search of his tracks, or of some gap in the foliage that would indicate what direction he had taken. But he had left no tracks that I could see. I was then overcome with a deep sadness. I felt abandoned and alone. I wasn't able to become one with this space yet, and much less with the whole jungle, as Cuatiendioy had advised.

Somewhere nearby, there was a stream flowing over some rocks. It generated an echo that spread over the surroundings. All around me, life was thriving abundantly. But I wasn't in the mood for contemplating anything. Everything annoyed me. 'Doing nothing is doing everything,' Cuatiendioy had told me. He had also said, 'Fortunate is the man who becomes capable of not doing anything, of not thinking about anything. Only in that state will he be able to understand the meaning of existence.'

I wasn't doing anything, but I was sad. I was aware of that and I needed to explore it. I remembered Cuatiendioy again, 'Nothing must stop you, Timoté. Not even a positive thought that amuses your mind. You will need to set it free. Nothing remains forever. If you stay in your past, or if you want to experience your future today, you lose. Here in the jungle, there can be no distractions.

I went out to contemplate the sun. Through gaps in the canopy of the jungle, I could see it rising. I knew it would shine on the ground only for a span of very few hours. It was a privilege to be able to contemplate it in that beautiful setting, so peaceful and quiet. Most of the days were spent under the shade cast by the immensely tall trees.

It was a day to evoke scenes from this long journey into nowhere, in the company of Cuatiendioy. I could see that each and every one of his words was a transmission of wisdom, just as the confrontations he generated were challenges he invited me to face, so that I could discover my own limitations.

Now, left to myself, I wondered how Cuatiendioy knew I was a fugitive fleeing from the army. Another question came to my mind: rather than being alone, in the middle of these strange surroundings, wouldn't it have been better to accept the sacrifice of serving in the army?

But I realized nothing could weaken my firm conviction that going back to military service was unacceptable. It would mean facing the risk of death, or of killing innocent civilians who had been captured by the guerrillas and forced to fight for them. There was no way I was prepared to do that. In that moment, I was no longer afraid of the army. But, of course, what army? There was no army to be afraid of here, in the heart of the Amazon jungle.

I tried to understand why I had become involved with that *indio,* and memories of different episodes in our relationship came back to my mind. *I remembered the day when the police were after me and I managed to hide in the forest. The doctors of the town where I lived disliked me because I treated patients with medicinal herbs so they reported me to the police as an "undesirable element." I had a clear picture in my mind of that place, where malaria took lives every day. This fact was the reason why I had first become interested in medicinal herbs. In one of those remote locations, as I was on my way home one evening, I saw a man lying on the ground right next to the road. He had clearly come down with malaria. Judging from his aspect, it wasn't likely that he could afford a doctor's fees and he didn't even have the strength to walk home. I drew up close to him and saw how sick he was. I asked for help from some passers-by and we carried him to my house. I covered him with the leaves from a plant called matarratón and gave him some gualanday tea. After an intense struggle with his fever, the man recovered. When I had first found him and held him in my arms, I felt I would be able to heal him. The intention in my heart was stronger than malaria. I had no doubt he would be cured. At the same time, I felt he was placing all his hopes in my arms. I had never before attempted to heal anyone, nor was it in my plans to become a healer. After one day of caring for him, the man recovered and expressed his gratitude as he left. Some days later, he came back with bananas and vegetables. He also brought his wife, who was suffering from another ailment.*

I didn't hesitate to receive her and see how I could help her. After expressing her gratitude for having healed her husband, she described the ailment she was suffering from, which had started after her son had been forcefully recruited by the guerrillas. I advised patience and suggested some plants that would soothe her nerves.

After only a few days, there was already a large number of patients waiting in line to see me. They would bring chickens, eggs, fruit, or vegetables. From being a fugitive, I had now become a healer. I didn't charge any fees but people brought all these foodstuffs as compensation for my services. This arrangement didn't last long. The town doctors put an end to it when they reported me to the police. In their eyes, I was a swindler and an usurper of the medical profession. I was taking away their customers who were humble but still left some money in the doctors' pockets.

One of my patients warned me that a complaint had been filed against me. I didn't want to have any trouble with the authorities, especially because it would entail the risk of having my real identity discovered. So I had to move away to another town. That was when I first met Cuatiendioy and invited him to have a glass of carambolo juice with me. Because of that glass of juice, here I was now, lost in the middle of the Amazon jungle.

At that point, while I remained wrapped up in my thoughts, I walked back to the *temascal*. I wanted to light a fire. I picked up the stones Cuatiendioy had left me and rubbed them together to produce a spark but they refused to work for me as easily as they did for him. Finally after multiple attempts, I managed to get the fire started. It was a nice fire, which gave off a warm glow. I poured some water into the bamboo pot, added some aromatic herbs to it, and prepared some delicious tea. I went out to sip it with deep enjoyment while taking in the beauty of the surroundings. I sat down to collect my thoughts and reflect on everything that had happened to me up to that moment. I wondered whether I would be able to find my way out of that place in the event that Cuatiendioy didn't come back. The truth was I had no idea what trail we had followed to enter this part of the jungle. It was a wide clearing, quiet, mysterious, and peaceful.

I realized it was getting late. It had been a day of reflection and solitude. I wasn't in the mood to light a fire outside. I wasn't hungry and I didn't feel like chewing that bitter *yuko* either.

With nightfall, the singing of birds came, the howling of monkeys, the croaking of frogs, and finally, the crickets chirping, fireflies glowing and the occasional hooting of an owl. Everything else slept. I was sitting on the trunk of a fallen tree, enraptured by the beauty of the night and gazing at the stars.

One day without Cuatiendioy had gone by. This would be the first night I would spend alone. I wondered what lesson this weird *indio* from the Amazon jungle had in mind for me. I was beginning to admit to myself that I felt deep affection for this *indio,* although his magical way of thinking about life was not my own way of thinking, and although his vision of life did not match what I had learned from my parents, from schools, and from books.

But I was there, according to Cuatiendioy, to forgive my past and to find my inner silence. As far as I was concerned, I didn't feel guilty about anything. And I would have to talk to myself. Otherwise, I could go insane. After a long while, everything became silent. I couldn't hear anything at all. Not even the usual chirping of the crickets. In that moment, when I tried to stand up and walk over to the *temascal*, I was pierced by a sharp pain in my backbone, and felt as if an electric current were circulating through my body. I lost control of my movements. In my pain, I cried out so loudly that I felt the echo would reverberate in the remotest corners of the jungle. I was paralyzed, frozen, as defenseless as a lost child. For an instant, I thought I could hear the jaguar very nearby. I visualized myself devoured by it, without being able to defend myself. Something strange was happening. Who could help me in this state of utter solitude and abandonment?

I tried to find some meaning or reason for that pain and remembered Cuatiendioy, who always said, "a pain is the response to a disharmony." I couldn't see anything. I didn't believe I had any disharmony. But the pain was getting more intense, and I felt lost. Likely to be devoured. I believed it was the last day of my life.

Overcome by the pain and the feeling of powerlessness, I curled up as I lay in the undergrowth. While I tried to figure out where the pain came from or whether I had made a bad movement and strained a muscle, scenes from my first eight years of life started coming to me, this time without Cuatiendioy touching my backbone with his hand. Now it was a connection with pain. It was something strange. *I remembered being at home with my parents, holding a sling in my hands, aiming at a hummingbird that was introducing its long beak into a lily, and hitting its fragile body with the stone I had hurled at it. I broke its wings. I could see it dying as I held it in my hands, defenseless, hurt, broken. It had still been alive when I picked it up but then it died.*

How could I have done that? How could I be so savage? I was in the scene again, facing my mother. She was scolding me severely, making me understand that it was evil to kill these defenseless creatures of the earth, or any other form of life. The pain was growing more and more intense and I still couldn't understand the nature of my suffering. I didn't know whether I hadn't forgiven myself for what I had done to the hummingbird, or whether it was nature that was making me pay for that incident or whether I had bought Cuatiendioy's idea that the earth makes us pay for everything.

Whatever it came from, the pain was intense and I was paralyzed. Innocently, I asked the hummingbird to forgive me or as Cuatiendioy said, I asked the consciousness of all birds to forgive me. I went on to ask forgiveness for everything because I didn't want to feel that pain any longer. I saw there was a clash between Cuatiendioy's teachings and my mother's. My mother said: "Ask God to forgive you. He forgives everything." But Cuatiendioy said, "The *civilized man* has a strange God that he himself invented. It's a God who is not just because the *civilized man* kills and also destroys himself and creates suffering for the earth. He believes he's immortal. He sees death only for the elderly. And what's worse, he doesn't even believe he's ever going to be elderly himself. And when he does think about growing old, he has confidence he can ask his God to forgive him at his deathbed. But the *indio* doesn't do that. He sees his God all the time and becomes one with Him."

Again I asked to be forgiven for everything I had ever done against nature and against my own nature. But it all seemed useless. I was in the middle of the jungle and there was another law here. I was under that law now.

Only when I was able to feel compassion for all of the birds locked up and mistreated in cages all over the world, I began to recover the ability to move. The pain gradually decreased. My mouth was dry. I felt an intense need to sleep. I looked towards the *temascal* and saw the fire had gone out. I badly wanted to go over to it so I could cuddle up and get some sleep, but I felt that the jaguar was observing me. I could sense its presence and felt defenseless. I tried to stand up swiftly and dash off running but I fell down on the ground like a sack full of stones. I felt my bones breaking and exclaimed, *Oh, God! Not yet! I don't want to die devoured by wild beasts.* The pain grew intense once more, and felt like a discharge of electricity down my spine. I was left nailed to the ground.

"Help me, Cuatiendioy!" That's all I managed. I had run out of strength. I had no voice. Again I had lost all capacity to move. I felt scared, trapped and sad, as if I were living the very last moments of my life. I thought I could feel the claws of the jaguar that would soon devour me mercilessly. I took deep breaths, trying to control the fear. I started rolling my eyeballs in all directions. I couldn't remember what Cuatiendioy had taught me about that. Memories from when I was nine years old came to my mind. I could see myself chasing a chicken. It was exciting to catch it and feel the animal's heart beating fast from fear. My delight was in having succeeded in catching it after the chase around the chicken coop. I experienced the scene clearly and after that, I could also taste the delicious broth, into which the chicken had been transformed. But my pleasant feelings didn't last long. Now I was the pursued party, not the pursuer. Now I was the one who felt weary, scared, powerless. Now I was the chicken. There wasn't much difference. Its fear was now my fear. I felt trapped.

Here again, I was under the law of the jungle, as Cuatiendioy said. Going back to the experience and clearing it up was my chance of obtaining forgiveness. I directed my gaze upwards and tried to understand my past by finding the connections between different events and making my peace with the pain. By then, the cold was becoming more intense and daybreak was drawing near. The monkeys were beginning with their screeching and gradually a few other noises were starting to be heard as well. I had spent the night outside of the *temascal*, in contact with my past and with the pain I had inflicted on nature. My own pain was slowly subsiding. I still felt numbness in my feet. I massaged them until they recovered their normal condition.

The morning started out in its usual manner, but I woke up feeling very strange as a result of these new bouts of pain. I thought maybe I would have to go through similar pain for each mistake I had made in my life. I didn't want that. I hadn't asked to come here in order to pay for my mistakes. What had this strange episode been about? Why had Cuatiendioy led me to that inner place? I had never asked him to do it. I didn't understand how the law of the *indio* worked. And I didn't want to understand it.

At school I had learned to think according to the principles of materialism. This teaching was not compatible with my way of thinking. I reflected about all this. But the fact was that I was there, and I had no one I could tell regarding all these strange things that were happening to me. They were mine and mine alone. Nobody else was concerned about the pain I suffered during those episodes. Nor was anyone else concerned with the whole experience I was going through. At that point, I began to remember other occasions when I had participated in actions against Nature.

Once a friend from Venezuela invited me over to his cattle ranch. The journey to the farm was pleasant, and so was my stay at the ranch. Until it was time for us to leave.

"We're leaving," my friend said. "But I need to take some cows to the slaughterhouse, so I'm going to load just a few of them onto the truck first and then we can set out."

"What do you mean? That wasn't the plan. You know it's something I don't like. I stopped doing it when I was child."

"Well, then, don't do anything if you don't want to. Don't help me. I need to take them, one way or another."

He came back with several laborers and they started loading the cows onto the truck, one at a time. Everything was going well until one of the cows put a leg in the gap between two boards and got stuck there. I tried to warn my friend but he paid no attention. He kept tugging at the cow with a rope he had tied to another car until he fractured its leg in three parts. I shouted at him repeatedly to stop but he just ignored my expressions of indignation. He only remarked, "It's on its way to the slaughterhouse, anyway. Spare me the sentimentality, will you? You'll be seeing it in a barbecue tomorrow." We set out towards the slaughterhouse but I got off some blocks before and found a taxi to take me the rest of the way.

I felt guilty and shocked. The following week, this same friend invited me over to his ranch again. I replied, "Never in my life!" And I kept my word ever since. My friend went off to the ranch, as usual. Less than thirty minutes had gone by when I got a phone call from his uncle. He asked me to go to the emergency room of the local clinic as quickly as I could because his nephew had had an accident. When I arrived, my friend was in surgery. He had fractured his leg so badly that metal pins were being implanted to hold the bone fragments together.

When I went into his room at the hospital to see him, I didn't feel sorry for his pain. Actually what his pain did was to connect me with the pain he had inflicted on the cow the week before. I saw clearly that the law of Nature was acting there. My friend didn't understand it at the time and probably doesn't understand it now either. He surely explains it away as a case of bad luck. Retrospectively, I could now have a better understanding of Cuatiendioy, his law and his God.

All those memories made me very sad. Many of them were accompanied by intense physical pain. By the time I had managed to process my past, it was already daytime. The jungle was silent. I had barely enough strength left to stand up. I walked to the *temascal,* entered into its warmth, and fell fast asleep. I don't know how long I slept. I was awakened by my hunger. I ate *yuko*, palm flower, seeds and *jimerita* honey. I went out to welcome the sun and started massaging my feet. I was sitting in a posture that was very similar to the lotus position. I didn't feel the presence of fear any longer. All around me there was no one. I also felt as if there was nothing either. I straightened up my spine, aligned my ears with my shoulders, fixed my gaze on a point in front of me, and tried to imitate Cuatiendioy. I made an effort to remember his teachings and to avoid thinking about what I was going through. I allowed everything to come to me, without clinging to anything. I felt a pleasant warmth moving up along my spine and my whole body was permeated with a new kind of energy. I don't know how long I remained in that posture. I only know that when I came in contact with my surroundings again, I felt profoundly at peace. I stood up effortlessly and went to get some water from the stream.

I searched for some berries so as to eat something other than *yuko*. It was late in the day. I searched all over and couldn't find anything. That was strange because Cuatiendioy had left me in a kind of paradise. Now it was all silent. There weren't any fruits or birds or insects to be seen. I collected some water from the stream and started walking back to the *temascal*. After a while, I had the impression the walk was taking too long. I believed I hadn't walked such a long distance when I had gone from the *temascal* to the stream. I began to feel tired and when I noticed it was getting dark, I got scared I wouldn't be able to find my way back to the clearing. I began to panic because it was almost nightfall and I was losing control over my body. I felt defeated, exhausted, and sad. I rebuked myself for having strayed away for so long. When it was finally nighttime, I pulled off some branches and leaves and found a place on a large tree. I felt the mysterious silence of the night, and missed the shelter of my tiny home in the jungle.

Cuatiendioy had told me we would go in search of my past, in order to find the clues of my life, but I hadn't seen a single clue so far. The only thing I experienced was a fear that I could feel in the uttermost atoms of my body. I began to review my past. *I remembered those delightful walks I had been on in the Andes mountain range when I was a child. I visualized myself side by side with my most beloved cousin and friend, Cristancho, who could embellish the most simple history into the most fascinating adventure, and every time he recounted the same history, it was as if you were listening to a new adventure. He was also my most valued friend and I had taken him as my role model. My cheerful cousin, who had the magic to make me see the green in the landscapes as if it were even greener, and to make me feel we were walking amidst the most beautiful landscapes of the Swiss Alps. He lived in the city but he would come to spend his vacations on our farm. I used to wait eagerly for his arrival. He had a special talent for flying kites and balloons. With his balloons, he taught me how to dream and how to fly. The balloons would go up in flames each time, shortly after he had released them into the air. These were special performances that took place before an audience made up of the laborers who joined me in admiring his crazy dreams. He wanted to send his balloons up to ever-increasing record-breaking heights on each occasion. My cousin was always telling me about his many adventures. As a result of the inspiration from his stories, I wanted to fly, just like his balloons. In our long walks in the Andes, contemplating some snowy peak, we didn't bring along anything to eat, but we never felt hungry. Within our shared silence, nothing else was needed. Maybe because peacefulness is such precious nourishment that it fills up much more than your stomach. My cousin was capable of making anyone who was around him feel good.* Right then, I wished he was there with me, keeping me company.

According to Cuatiendioy, any event of my life that repeatedly came to my mind could be an indicator pointing towards some clue. But in that moment, I could see nothing but the adventures. I spent all night long visualizing episodes of my life but I couldn't identify a single clue in connection with them. Daybreak came and the jungle was still silent. There were no birds singing. Everything seemed empty. I tried exploring the jungle a bit, in the hope of finding some insect, but there was nothing. I started searching for the way back to the clearing. I followed my own tracks along a trail, but the more I walked, the more I felt I was straying further away from the *temascal*.

I pulled off one of my bootlaces and tied it on a branch, as a signal. At times, I thought I had found the way back to the point where Cuatiendioy and I had come into the jungle. So I would ask myself, *What could be better than to have Cuatiendioy find me back in the town?* But that wasn't to be. It was only my dream of going back. I was lost in the heart of the Amazon jungle. After a long walk in the surroundings, I found the bootlace I had tied on a branch. I said to myself, *Oh, my God! I've been walking in circles!* I retrieved my bootlace and set out in a different direction. I noticed the volume of water in the little stream had increased. I concluded it must have rained somewhere else and calmed down a little. I took my clothes off and got into the stream, holding my clothes up with one hand. I floated along with the current. I avoided getting entangled in any branches and continued floating in search of a shallower part of the stream. I tested its depth every few minutes, and on my third try I found it was shallow enough for me to walk, the water coming up only to my waist. Finally, I climbed out of the stream and continued my search on foot. By then, it was getting late. I was scared again. I felt I needed to sit down to rest a little and decide what direction to follow. It was almost nightfall. What I wanted was a nice place where I could rest. I stumbled over a fallen tree trunk and fell on my haunches. The trunk was covered with mushrooms and it was so rotten that it had become a sticky mass. When I tried to stand up, the excruciating pain in my spine came back and kept growing worse. I couldn't move. I couldn't feel my heartbeats. I felt as if my blood was not circulating. I felt my flesh sagging. I wanted to understand what was happening to me. I tried looking upwards but found only emptiness there. Below, there was only my pathetic self. To my left, I perceived myself, observing the scene. I had a perception of myself in two separate parts, and I asked myself, *'Who is this other self of mine?'*

One part of me felt uneasy and full of fear. The other part was calm and peaceful. I wanted to change my body for another one, but I couldn't. I had to remain in this one. My True *Self* could not fit into another body because it would become rigid and compact. In that body, I was nothing. There was no rhythm there and it was cold. I was in neither of the two bodies, but I still felt I was alive. I tried looking within my body and found it was empty. There was no form in it. I went to the other body and saw it was a petrified self. My first body was nothing. It was neither bone nor flesh. It was the rotten tree trunk or the sticky mass. It was soil, it was mud, or it was the leaf that dropped to the ground, it was the hanging *liana*. It was everything and it was nothing.

That was how I spent the night. I don't know how long I remained in that state of despair. I could no longer distinguish between dreaming, reality, hallucination and nightmare. I just wanted my body to recover so I could get back to the *temascal*; otherwise I was going to die here, trapped in the jungle. After an intense struggle, I was able to make contact with my body. I felt neither cold or weariness. The sun was shining on my head and subtle beams of warmth touched my back. As I felt no pain, I thought I was dead. Finally, I managed to stand up and began walking. I felt neither cold or pain. I made contact with my body again and had the perception that I was inwardly lost, entangled, not flowing with life. I was a fugitive, a deserter from the army. But looking back, I saw that in the city I had also been lost. I had hidden my sensibility under the noise and the excitement of the cement jungle. The mere idea of thinking about the city sent a chill of disgust down my spine. *I remembered the sadness I felt when I first had to leave the countryside and move to the city. It hadn't been easy leaving the green landscapes of my childhood even when it was to continue my education. I was the son of simple country folks who had no malice or trickery in them, so they had not passed any of those traits to me. We led a simple life on the farm. There were no luxuries. There was no electric light. We had a battery-powered radio, but being in the middle of the Andes mountain range, there was a very limited number of radio signals that we could tune into.*

I remembered that when I was a child, feelings were our only means of communication. Every evening, my mother would pray to God for her sons who were away from home. I would sit next to her and pray to God that my elder brothers would bring me toys when they came home to visit us. God did protect my brothers and they did bring me toys, so my magical thoughts came true.

This could be attributed to mere coincidence but for a child it was very real. Sitting down to pray that a wish might come true worked so well for me that I continued with this practice for many years, even when I was a student at university. It stopped when I fell under the influence of materialist ideology.

I felt now was the moment for me to reflect on the simple details of life. Cuatiendioy had told me: "Beauty is in simple things." and he urged me to see beyond external forms. He also said once, "Forms are empty. Seek in the emptiness of forms." At the time, I had no idea what he was talking about. To me, he was just a weird *indio*, who appeared to be spaced out most of the time but sometimes seemed able to read my thoughts. He rarely spoke but it was delightful to be with him. I loved the way he prepared the herbs for his prescriptions and how he spoke about their healing properties. On one occasion, while he was rolling one of the numerous balls he made with his medicinal herbs, he fixed his penetrating gaze on me, as if he were looking into my very soul and said, "Oh, Timoté! It's great that you feel so lost. That's a good thing for the soul of a *civilized man*, because he always believes he's fine, when the truth is that he is lost. No matter what you do, some day you'll see all of this clearly."

It was already very late. I was still lost and with no idea of what direction to follow. I felt the need to find out if I'd recovered my voice, and shouted out as loudly as I could. I was also hoping Cuatiendioy might hear me, wherever he was. After doing this several times without any response, I picked up a large green leaf and used it to write down what was flowing out from my heart:

May the night not fall
before I reach the end of this tunnel,
this deep opening,
this far off yearning,
Oh, anguished crossing towards nothingness,
may the moon not come out
seeking for this shadow.
May the felled tree not shout out
vanquished trails.
Oh, anguished crossing towards nothingness,
do not call for me now.
I seek in the garden of earthly delights
for the intoxicating perfume of the lotus flower.
Not so late,
for I fear the shadow,
my shadow, my Self.
Lost in the dream of this journey,
It is with the full moon that I want to set out.
Awake,
lighthearted, and calm.
All and nothing:
Insubstantial passenger,
Irreplaceable traveler towards the night.

Shouting out, no matter what, helped me verify that I was still alive. Getting in touch with my feelings, writing or creating fantasies in my mind, gave me a kind of peacefulness. But soon I'd go back to feeling anger. How was it possible that I couldn't find the clearing, the *temascal*, when I hadn't strayed so far? How could I be so clumsy and not find it when it was so near the stream?

I tried again walking in the direction I believed would lead me to the *temascal*. I was sure I'd find it just a few steps further along the trail. I had just set out on my search again when suddenly I noticed there was unusual movement in all of the treetops. A strange kind of wind began swaying the solid branches and their exuberant foliage. It grew stronger and stronger and in a matter of seconds, the silence of the jungle was broken by its loud whistling. Every time I tried to walk forward, the wind literally pushed me back against the trees, and prevented me from making any progress. I looked for shelter amongst the bushes and remained there for a long while. I wanted to come out from the thicket but the wind kept me back. I looked for shelter again. That was another day I was going to spend deep in the jungle, away from the *temascal*. There was always some obstacle that made it impossible for me to find it.

While I waited for the wind to subside, I got in touch with the memory of an event from my childhood. I was walking to school one morning, alone and deep in my thoughts, as usual. The sky was overcast, grey and dull. There was an eerie atmosphere of uneasiness. The livestock were alert and restless. The ants were all moving in the same direction, neatly forming an orderly line. The buzzards were flying at a higher altitude than they normally did and they weren't gliding randomly. They were all flying in the same direction. Curiously, an owl was watching me closely. It was perched on the corrugated tin roof of a smoking shed. It stared at me as if it were trying to convey a message. I felt these were all clear signs that something was about to happen. Just then, a violent gust of wind, maybe the tail-end of a hurricane, swept me up into the air. All my notebooks flew away into the air above the meadow. I landed about fifty meters away from where I had been lifted up. It was rough and frightening when I hit the ground, but I wasn't really injured. All I got were a few scratches. I stood up and ran for cover. I found a leafy coffee tree and sat down under its branches, while huge raindrops fell all around me.

All sorts of experiences I had in the jungle would take me back to my childhood, to the simplicity and depth I had lost through reason and logic. Cuatiendioy would have said, "Why didn't you listen to the message from the cows, or from the owl? Why didn't you follow the example of the ants?" Whether as a child or as an adult, it was the same: I was afraid then and I was still afraid now, and in the present moment, it was also necessary to pay attention to all of the messages nature had sent me.

Cuatiendioy once said, "All the different peoples, everywhere in the world, are in communication with one another. And their communication was better before the *white men* arrived. The feeling of the *Indio* is one and the same from the North to the South, and sometimes his communication reaches beyond continents. It's like radio waves, Timoté. Just as some of my fellow *indios* don't understand the *civilized man's* communications, *white men* don't understand the *indio's* communication. We all have messengers for the moments when we have ceased feeling. All of the *indios'* messengers are here together in the Amazon jungle. That's why we need to save it. Here, every group or tribe makes a covenant with a messenger. The *tecolote* owl is the messenger of death for the North. With its song, it announces when it's time for an *indio* to depart, to die. For the South, the black-winged night moth announces to the family members that there will be a death that day. For your people, it's the *tres pies* bird, or striped cuckoo. There are many other messengers, Timoté; but you're going to have to discover them for yourself."

On this occasion, during my experience with the wind, I came to see the relevance of all those events from my childhood that kept coming to my mind. I wondered whether those beliefs most people call "superstitions" might have a meaning, and whether I might discover it some day. But all those thoughts would have to wait. What I needed right now was to rest.

In the midst of these settings, and being in utter solitude, I was able to come face to face with some memories from my childhood and to relive my past. I was still full of fears, but the very concept of death had changed for me. Now, dying had acquired a new dimension. Thinking about this change filled me with peacefulness. At the same time however, I didn't want to die in this solitary setting. I wanted to be at peace with life at the moment of my death. I wanted to be certain that my perceptions were not an illusion. Meanwhile the wind blew over the exhuberant treetops, like a caress to their green, leafy branches. First it shook off their drier leaves, which dropped down to the ground and covered my feet. Gradually, as it began to blow more intensely, the weaker green leaves also started to drop, forming a multi-colored tapestry, typical of Fall, when they reached the ground.

I felt there was something I couldn't afford to miss. Somehow, I *knew* that I couldn't let that "something" pass me by and leave me behind. I had to try to grasp it, to manifest it in a material space, to shout it out, to release it so that it wouldn't choke me, or die in my silence. It was something that mingled with my anguish, something that cried out to be set free. In the midst of my despair, I sought relief in writing this on a tree bark:

> *The weather sways back and forth*
> *with langurous sighs.*
> *The doomed leaves*
> *dart out from the heights*
> *and delicately fluttering,*
> *drop down to the ground*
> *as if they were mortal creatures*
> *with grey burial shrouds,*
> *with green burial shrouds,*
> *with white burial shrouds.*
> *They glide down like melancholy birds,*
> *Featherless, their wings broken,*

like a troupial singing
its tinny sounding song.
Autumn is an elderly man,
who clutches to the corpses of the dead
and amidst his mixed-up prayers,
buries them for the cruel winter.

Everything happened strangely. I was out of reality, maybe because I had eaten so little, and because of the coldness of the jungle and my body, the harsh winter I felt in my soul and my cold hands holding the tree bark on which I was pouring out my sorrow.

I don't know how long it took me to write down my ravings. In my trance, I found myself hoping all this was a bad dream. But it wasn't. I was there, within my body, which I was trying to lead back to the *temascal*. All I had to do was cross the stream but in my weakened condition, I kept seeing it further and further away. I had never experienced a perception of distance like the one I had in that moment. Distance became, for me, the degree of difficulty in reaching a place. My feet felt heavy and I found it hard to walk forward. Overwhelmed by frustration at my incompetence in finding the *temascal,* I wanted to give up, but when I looked down to the ground I noticed that, right next to my feet, the ants were all marching in the same direction. I concluded that a storm was approaching.

The ants moved quickly, bearing their burdens of leaves and twigs. I kept my eyes on them until I saw them go into the hollow of a tree. Right then, I realized that the tree where the ants lived would remain above water when the stream overflowed. I tried to climb onto it but I couldn't find a branch within my reach and the trunk was too thick for me to climb by locking my arms and legs around it. It was so large that it would take more than five men to encircle it. If only I could climb it, that tree would be the best place to spend the night. As that proved impossible, I decided to remain under its shadow.

It felt as if I were in the middle of a nightmare again. The stream overflowed, the raindrops grew larger, and then it started hailing. The hailstones beat against the trees and tore down their leaves. A raging storm had broken out. Bolts of lightning kept falling nearer and nearer and the claps of thunder were deafening. The spaces between one thunderbolt and the next were moments of agonizing suspense. At one point I began bidding farewell to everything: my body, my parents, my brothers, relatives and friends.

The flood overran everything in its path. Although the storm was over after only a short while, every second of it seemed an eternity to me. Before the storm had ended, the jungle was already completely flooded. Clearly, reaching the *temascal* would be impossible now. In that moment, thinking about the *temascal* felt like thinking about a huge mansion.

I was cold. I felt the urgent need to light a fire. I remembered my two flintstones and in that moment I considered them to be my most valued possession. I would trade any other wealth in the world for those valuable stones. They were back in the *temascal*, which felt at the same time so near and so far away.

On the ground right beneath that huge tree, I piled up some branches and constructed a kind of den. Then I drew a circle around it and asked for permission from the jungle, silently repeating, "This is my space," just as I had learned from Cuatiendioy. I also remembered him saying, "Everything is in the mind, Timoté. When there are no noises in it, all the creatures in nature obey it."

My clothes were cold and damp. I took them off and wrapped myself in some leaves. I surrendered my skinny body to the roots of that beautiful tree, which seemed to feel my heart, and at the same time opened up its own heart to me, protecting me like a mother protects her child. Rather than lost in the Amazon, I was lost within myself.

I reflected upon the fact that I had spent most of my life running, in a hurry, with little or no moments devoted to contemplation. No one had ever taught me to see, much less to feel. I was now experiencing a state in which I was able to see and to feel. I felt naked in every sense. I snuggled up, adopting the posture of a baby. I was cold and didn't want to think about anything. I let go of thinking about my body and yielded to the calmness of the night. I felt my heartbeats as never before. Beyond my body there was the wind. Only the wind and a deep silence. And a call for my body to become one with the beloved earth. I, the witness of my own death.

In this almost poetic state, I could see a cold, frozen and defenseless body, curled up in fetal position. In this same state and as a witness of my own body, I could see insects arriving, crawling over my face up to my eyes, going in through my nostrils, inspecting me all over. As they perceived a total absence of movement, they sent out their message throughout the jungle. Hundreds, and even thousands of insects steadily arrived. Some of them used their sharp jaws to bite into my fragile body. Others injected strange substances into it. Some of the insects that appeared had strange features such as I had never seen before in my life. And it was precisely my life that had to return to its starting point. I was the protagonist of my own film, and, at the same time, the audience watching it.

Here, on this occasion, my senses were so present and sharp that I could hear in the distance, the sounds I had once heard while walking alongside Cuatiendioy, the sounds of some familiar ants coming up to inspect my cold, rigid body. One of them crawled up to my nose and gave a shrill, high-pitched cry that the other ants repeated. Instantly there was an outburst of noises throughout the jungle. An army of ants marched up to the spot where my body was and injected a strange liquid into me, which made my body tasty for them. From then on, wholesale looting broke out. Each insect took its share of me. I was being carried away by strange insects and becoming part of them. I traveled inside my sister ant, in the fly, in the beetle, in the ladybug, in the buzzard's beak, in the wild dog who tore me to pieces and spread my remains through the dank jungle. From being bread to the ants, I morphed into the anteater hunted by the eagle and next I was the eagle's flight. From being inside beetles, I passed into the troupial's beak. I was its beautiful song. From being the fly and its larvae, I became the spider, knitting its deadly traps; I was its silken thread which caught insects, that dropped down back on the ground, lifeless. The tree roots would catch them and turn them into sap, which flowed upwards to the treetops. I became a tree. I was the whole living jungle. And I was nothing. Infinite ecstasy, with no observer, no self, the perfect abode, the divine origin, with neither beginning nor end.

But it was not my time yet. A warm beam of light filtered through the foliage, caressing my body. It was the newly risen sun, dazzling my eyes.

"Oh my God!" I cried. "I'm alive!"

I came out from my makeshift shelter, aching and stiff all over, my body almost lifeless and thoroughly bitten and stung by insects. The jungle had a newly found charm for me now. I walked to the stream and laid out my clothes to dry on a large rock. I didn't want to think about anything, just to feel life.

I spent a long time sitting next to the rock until my clothes were dry. Finding the *temascal* wasn't so important for me anymore. I wasn't afraid. Any place was fine to go on living. I could let the days go by without worrying about time. What mattered was knowing that I was alive and that life was giving me a chance to become one with the jungle and with myself. I felt an overwhelming need to write. I found a colored stone and used it to write on the rock:

> *Only during some evenings,*
> *the wind blows off me*
> *some dead phrases, like leaves*
> *that you never knew were in me.*
> *Only for one instant,*

the fragile lines of a poem
run through my veins,
replacing my blood
with only a subtle memory.
But, oh! the dead hours,
the screams and my sorrows,
just as in the withered evenings
that fill me with pain,
bringing me a memory,
just barely a memory.
Life is a gentle breeze
that sometimes bursts out of control
and brings with it, in a poem,
a few good phrases.
Life is a bitter wind
when it nourishes grief.
Life is an instant,
just barely an instant.

When I finished writing I had a feeling of joy. Not because
I felt the poem was valuable, but because I had allowed myself to

write it with no fear of how others might judge it. It was so free and open and at the same time, so complete in itself. It would remain there, on that rock, although no one would ever read it. Something good about these experiences in the jungle was that they were empowering me to cry out, or to write down, what I used to call "my poems" when I was child. I remembered showing them to my teacher at school, and always going away with the feeling that he didn't approve of them. I understand him now. His reasoning was different from mine. I dared to write whatever, with no respect for semantics or rhythm. What I was doing now was also another way of releasing my trivial frustrations. The scent of the jungle grew more and more intense.

All the suffering I had undergone in the past also seemed trivial to me now. None of the things that had worried me before in my life seemed to have any relevance when I compared them to what I had just been through. I had no idea how many days had gone by, but the *temascal* no longer seemed important, nor did the flintstones. I had forgotten the taste of food. All I needed was water to stay alive. That was enough for the time being. The scent of the jungle grew. I could see beautiful colors in the water of the stream. I could hear it gurgling as it flowed. There was no other sound for me at that moment.

Sitting on the rock, I straightened up my spine and aligned my ears with my shoulders. I wanted to connect, to come back to reality, to find the peacefulness that pervades when there is silence.

I had a clear perception of the degree of exhaustion and weakness of my body. At the same time, I was more in a dream-like daze than in contact with reality. In this state, I would drift off into memories of events that connected me with the source of some pain or other. I had finally bought into Cuatiendioy's idea that (as he had said), "One needs to go deep within the pain until one finds its source." Although it was clear to me that, at one level, my recent experiences during the storm were the reason why my body was aching all over, I still felt curious as to whether there might also be a different origin for those pains.

Then I remembered one morning, during my travels with Cuatiendioy, when we passed through a small village where people knew the indio was a healer. There were already a large number of patients waiting in line to see him. Cuatiendioy sat down before them and after inspecting them closely one by one, he selected those who had the most serious ailments and handed out the medicinal herb that each one of them required. I helped him out on that occasion, organizing and handing over to him the herbs he needed. That morning, there was an elderly man standing in the line who kept crying out in pain. I gently pulled him out of the line and made him lie down on a mat right in front of Cuatiendioy. Cuatiendioy looked him over for only a second and said, "Not this one!"

"But how come? He's the sickest of all."

"Precisely, Timoté. This one can't be cured with herbs. His illness is of the soul, and pain is the cure. He will be able to heal on his own when he understands the cause of his pain."

"Tell him, Cuatiendioy."

"No, Timoté, it would be useless. If a piece of advice could be of any use, this man would already be free from pain."

I was really puzzled by his reply, so I tried to find out about this elderly man's past. I asked some of the other patients about his life. Most of them had little information but there was another elderly man who told me a long story about the man's past. He had been a vicious murderer during war time when he was young.

According to Cuatiendioy, that man would have to reach a state of awareness in which he could find the origin of his pain and forgive himself for his past.

In the course of remembering this story, I realized I needed to discover the origins of my own pain. So I began to search amidst the wreckage of my memories. I found feelings connected with the pain I had caused my loved ones when I disappeared from their lives. I also found feelings concerning the romantic attachments I had made with a couple of women to whom I had sworn eternal love. When I reached a state of fully conscious awareness of the pain I had caused with my actions, the pain went away. And then I felt I loved that pain. Any pain was nothing, compared to what I had just been through.

I resumed contact with my body and regained control over it. Slowly, I began to shift my posture. When I opened my eyes, I saw a different jungle. Everything was alive. I felt I was in Paradise. The orchids had a special glow about them. The gurgling stream conveyed its fluid movement to all of the surroundings. There were butterflies with beautifully colored wings all around. I walked towards the stream and crossed over to the other side. I wasn't worried about finding the clearing any longer or the *temascal* either.

VI

The Return Of Cuatiendioy

I couldn't believe it! I had been lost for so long, and I had been only on the other side of the stream all that time. How could I have been so clumsy and gone through all that suffering, when I had been so near to a place of safety?

I felt the impact of seeing so many animals gathered together in the specific spot I was observing. There were parrots in that place, macaws, toucans, monkeys, tapirs, *lapas*, deer and armadillos, all basking in the sun. I thought maybe I was in heaven, and God was hiding in the foliage of the jungle, to avoid witnessing man's shame for the iniquities he has perpetrated as a result of straying so far from nature, and therefore from himself.

The animals could share that space with no fear, no expectations and no violence. As I watched them closely, I had the impression they were telling me, "Do something for the jungle!" and I was filled with sorrow for all I had not done, for my insensibility towards life and for my lack of respect for the natural world. I grieved for the animals in zoos, locked up in those gruesome cages. I felt a deep sadness for how poorly our education prepares us to understand wildlife and for the misconceptions I had assimilated from my teachers and from society at large. I could hear every bird screaming into my ears, "Do something for those who are suffering in cages! There are no compassionate ears to hear their prayers."

As I gradually got closer to the *temascal,* I felt each of those animals was touching my soul. I was overwhelmed by feelings of guilt and sadness. I wept when I recognized the animal within me and saw my arrogance in believing I was superior to them. I saw myself as a despot, an insensitive and absurd king. I could see there was a creature of the wilderness within me, and that nature had never parted from me. I was the one who had gone away from it.

I also saw the difference between those creatures of the jungle and myself, in the way we related to one another. It was as if they were always able to understand me when they looked into my eyes, but I couldn't understand their messages. Still, in spite of my clumsiness, I felt that in the context where I was now, I was able to communicate with them and understand them.

My energies were directed towards reaching the *temascal* now. In my imagination, I could already see the campfire and the smoke rising up from it. After taking a long look at the surroundings, I turned my gaze towards the *temascal.* To my amazement, there was a jaguar lying right in front of its entrance. I hadn't yet recovered from my amazement when I heard, "What are you waiting for, Timoté? Come on in, or I'll enjoy this delicious hot tea without you."

"Cuatiendioy! When did you get here?"

"What does it matter? Just come inside."

"What about the jaguar?"

"You really *are* crazy, Timoté. He's been at your side all this time. Don't you recognize him?"

"Not with me. I was alone."

"All right. Come inside. We'll talk about that later."

I had to pass very close to that beautiful jaguar in order to get into the *temascal.* He seemed more like a gentle pet than a dangerous wild animal. As soon as I was inside the *temascal,* I smelled the scent of herbs and it filled up all the space around us. Cuatiendioy was sitting as he always did, with his legs crossed in lotus position, his backbone straight, his gaze deep and peaceful, his warm, open smile, through which his gold tooth could be seen. He looked at me and said, "Well, then, Timoté. How does one feel after six months in the jungle, feeding on fruit, roots, leaves, and *yuko*? And with nine days of fasting and drinking only water?"

"But, how's that, Cuatiendioy? Have you been away so long?"

"I hope it's been long enough for you to start getting acquainted with the jungle."

"So then, all this has been a trick of yours?"

"Take it any way you like," he said. Then he fell silent.

I couldn't recover from my amazement. I was speechless, lost in my efforts to process this shock. Suddenly, Cuatiendioy spoke, "It's time to celebrate your achievements. You'll need to eat well in order to set out on our journey again."

He laid two large leaves on a rock. On one of them, he placed some cornmeal buns he had been warming up over the campfire. On the other leaf, he placed a bamboo bowl filled with a delicious hot tea. The table was set. There was nothing missing. Enjoying the taste of the tea and the buns after nine days of fasting was enough to send me into ecstasy. A cornmeal bun, in these circumstances, was far more than a cornmeal bun. It was an exquisite delicacy. First, I took in the pleasure of this wonder through my eyes. I feasted on its essence before holding it in my hands and physically eating it. I did the same with the tea, before drinking it.

I had never realized the sacred nature of our food. I felt ashamed of the way I had been used to eating in the past. Cuatiendioy ate silently. There would be plenty of time later to exchange stories about our experiences.

"Eat another bun. My wife told me to let you have two if I found you alive."

"Thanks. And how are they all? Your family?"

"They're fine. I don't need to visit them to know all is well with them. I only visit because I like to spend time with them. During my travels, I have my messengers and they bring me news about my family."

I felt happy knowing I was no longer on my own. I started calculating the time that had gone by, and I asked, "Tell me, Cuatiendioy, have we been in the jungle for six months already?"

"Sure, just take a look at your things. Actually, wash your clothes! They stink to high heaven. Look at the sweat stains!"

Until that moment, I hadn't noticed the appalling condition of the clothes I was wearing. It had rained I don't know how many times while I was lost and I had never been been able to manage a change of clothes. The last occasion when I'd been in the *temascal* was the day before Cuatiendioy's departure. I wanted to tell him about all this, but I sensed he wasn't interested. Actually, when I tried to tell him all about it while I was bathing in the stream, he changed the subject.

"Each experience, Timoté, is unique and different. The tests are always the same ones, but each individual experiences them acording to what they need to learn. No one can really care about this, except your own spirit. Remembering in order to feel and to learn is living. Don't tell me about anything because no matter how hard you try, there's no way you'll be able to make me live your experience. I can understand what you experienced, but I will never be able to feel what you felt. Now, go wash your clothes, and be careful not to pollute the water. Remember that respect for the water and for the jungle are what matters most.'

By then, my perception of water and of the jungle had already changed. And every day I had a deeper understanding of the difference between looking and seeing.

"Now is the moment, Timoté. Learn how to listen because what you have been doing up to now has been just perceiving noises. If you carry on with your own noises and with other people's noises, you will lose yourself in them. Noises are the traps where the *civilized man* got lost. And this has made it impossible for him to understand both the *indio* and Mother Nature.

I listened to Cuatiendioy attentively. I especially wanted him to speak because it had been quite some time since I'd heard anyone's voice. And no one had heard my voice, except the jungle. Before his absence, I hadn't really appreciated the depth of his wisdom and wondered how he could possibly have acquired it. I found this puzzling because I suspected he didn't even know how to read.

I drew near to him, and looking him in the eye, I asked, "Cuatiendioy, where did you learn the things you know?"

"Right here," he replied.

"All right. This is where you learned about plants and animals. But how come you know all about the *civilized man*?"

"All right Timoté. This is going to be complicated for you to understand but I'll explain it to you all the same. It's time for you to learn something. Once you learn how to feel, you'll be able to discover on your own all the rest there is to know. *Becoming one with everything.* That's the key factor, Timoté. If I want to find out what a *civilized man* is like inside, I just imitate him and become one with him. Nothing exists separately. And none of us are separate from others. We are all one and the same force. Every single thought corresponds to an energy that changes according to the type of thought. Thoughts, just the same as feelings, travel like the wind does through the jungle. Can you see the wind? Of course you can't. All you can see is what it does when it pushes against everything in its path, against the trees, the leaves. You can also feel it when it brushes over your skin. That's how feelings and thoughts travel. All you need to do is just go into that void, and you'll find all the answers you need. That's why fear is poisonous. The cities are full of fear. *White men* run all the time without knowing why. And they travel at such high speeds with no idea of where to go."

"Why does that happen?"

"It's easy to understand. A child imitates his or her parents and eventually ends up being just like they are, thinking just like they do, eating just like they do, and even sometimes dying in the same way they do. Grown ups, in turn, cannot see other things because they have no time to speak with the Spirit of the earth, nor with the Spirit of the plants, much less do they have the time to feel the waves traveling like the wind and passing through their bodies. That's why they stick to what they learn in their schools. And thus they grow up, and thus they die, always searching outside themselves.

"Copying everything there is outside is very easy, but it generates a lot of suffering. I observe the *white men* whenever I travel. I seek out the wisest of them and get close to him. I imitate his movements and try to concentrate on his thoughts and on his feelings. The *civilized man* always has noise inside. He's always talking to himself, anxious, fearful. But I try to get into his luminous field.

"A man of knowledge moves within another field of energy. It's like the places where a shaft of sunlight reaches down into the jungle. Do you like places where there is sunlight? Of course you do! We all like those places. We just need to know where the clearing is. There is light in those spaces and there is also a special kind of warmth. But the rest of the jungle is cold. Sometimes it's all tangled up, like the *civilized man's* mind. And it's very cumbersome, Timoté. That's why I want you to leave behind that cumbersome and dark part of your mind, the one that brings you so much pain.

"A man of knowledge enters into a magical field, where he can make every dream come true, and he can transform what is impossible into what is possible. Well, then. I imitate those wiser *white men* I mentioned before, until I can get into their spaces of emptiness. They don't realize what I'm doing. They think I'm just another *indio*, in the same way that for the *civilized man*, a tree is only a tree and an animal is only an animal. They ignore me, while all the time I'm learning about what they have in their spaces of light. It's easy, Timoté. Does a deer need to ask the sun for warmth when it stops at a sunlit space in the jungle? Of course not. The sun simply sends warmth to it whenever the deer enters into one of its spaces of light, just like when I get inside the thoughts of a *civilized man* who happens to be wise.

A thought, Timoté, is a vibration, like the wind blowing through the trees. The stronger the wind, the greater the effect we can see on the leaves. A thought has its own shape, and it is always alive. All you need to do is search for it in the midst of silence. And you can see more than just its shape if you become one with it. It's all there. Everything lies dormant in the house of silence. That's why you need to be careful with your thoughts. When thoughts are accompanied by feeling, they enter into those luminous spaces I mentioned. And if there are also good intentions present, and there are energies in them, the magic will be even greater. You will never again be the same as you were in the past. You'll be a strange man amongst *white men*. You won't be able to find words to express what you are experiencing, because the knowledge you now have doesn't form part of the *civilized man's* knowledge."

"You mean you can read my thoughts?

"Sometimes, Timoté.When I imitate you."

"So then, why do you live like an *indio*? You could be acknowledged as a wise man."

"And what for, Timoté? Who would care about an *indio* who thinks differently, who feels differently or who dresses differently? If the *indio* were important for the *civilized man, the civilized man* wouldn't destroy the *indio's* environment. He wouldn't impose his beliefs on him. He wouldn't invade his land. The *white men* would listen to the messages from the *Curacas* and comply with them. Then the earth would reveal its secrets to all humans. The earth also has its spaces through which different vibrations travel. I've told you many times that the earth is an organism that is as much alive as your own heart is. The spaces that surround it are the same ones as yours or mine. To enter into the earth's spaces of sensitivity means living in places where the earth protects us and provides us with everything we need for our subsistence, with no effort required from us. The earth has other spaces that the *civilized man* can't see and that the *Curaca* knows."

"What, or who, is a *Curaca*?

"A *Curaca* is the chief of an indigenous community. They are the rulers, the wise men of the jungle, who teach the secrets of life and of the earth. They enter into the greatest spaces of silence. That's why they know more. The wiser the *Curaca* is, the more peaceful and full of wisdom life in his community will be. A *Curaca* first travels out of from his body and dwells in spaces of higher sensitivity. So, just as I learn by becoming one with the *civilized man*, the Curaca enter into other luminous spaces, and ask for guidance regarding what is best for the good of the community.

"A *Curaca* is a wise man. He knows about the healing powers of plants. He can talk with them and respects them. He also talks with the rain, negotiates with the wind, and knows nature intimately. He is prepared before his birth by the elderly Curacas, who come from other regions, days before He is born, and walk in circles around the hut or the *temascal* to protect Him.

"This practice existed until very recently. It stopped when the *white men* began persecuting these wise men and they had disperse in the jungle. The *Curacas* knew the *white men* were bringing many good things with them, but also some very bad ones. The ones from the North opened up to the *white men* and they were despised by them. Their lands were taken away from them; they were cheated, tortured and murdered. The ones from the South managed to keep something hidden. Some of them refused to have any contact with the *civilized man*. They are the ones who still have that which you find so strange—the *indio's* knowledge.

"The *white men* never understood us. They weren't capable of seeing or listening, much less of feeling. They polluted everything with the noise from their minds. They caused everything to be forgotten. They exterminated many messengers. Nowadays the only *Curaca* left is Tandioy, the chief or king of the Amazon. I'm only a messenger; a bridge beween the *indio* and the *civilized man*."

"Can I ask you about Tandioy?"

"I need to get permission to be able to talk with you about him."

"Who can grant that permission?"

"Only *he* can. But don't keep on getting entangled in this. Some day you'll know. Remember that time is only an entertainment in the *civilized man's* mind. Your mind exists due to everything you see, and everything you see exists because of your mind."

"I still don't understand, Cuatiendioy!"

"I know. Gather up your things. We're leaving now."

"Where are we going?"

"We're traveling forward. We've already traveled to the past. And it's time for you to find an ally, a messenger."

"What's a messenger?"

"Something like your pet, Toto. And your horse."

"Who told you I once had a horse?"

"No one. I guessed it. And don't ask any more questions. Find yourself another messenger friend."

"Do you have one already?

"Of course. I've got several"

"Where are they? Why don't I see them?"

"I know, Timoté. You aren't able to see yet."

I remembered about the jaguar and supposed it would be him. I looked around but it was nowhere to be seen. We dismantled the *temascal*, buried the cinders and cleaned up the surroundings. It made me sad to tear down what had been my home for a short time, my castle of leaves, my safety. We gathered our few belongings, including the precious flint stones we used for starting the fire. Cuatiendioy tightened up his sandals a bit, and hung his *ixtle* fiber bag with its strap diagonally across his back. He heaved a gentle sigh, whistled to the wind, turned in the direction that was opposite to the one I was expecting us to follow, and said, "This way. Follow my footseps. Keep your gaze straight ahead of you. It's time to feel the jungle."

I set out slowly, trying to understand what he had often said about *copying*. On some previous occasions, he had instructed me to follow the tracks he left behind while he continued striding ahead. At first, I had found it very difficult to coordinate everything at the same time and avoid thinking. I was expected to find a balance between the swinging of my hands and the movement of my feet with each step forward I took, while at the same time, keeping my backbone straight and looking directly ahead without getting distracted. And I was supposed to feel. All I felt was weariness and pain but Cuatiendioy urged me to seek for the feeling I had experienced on a few occasions. The problem was that such feeling appeared very rarely for me. For him it was normal, but to me it seemed as something deeper, almost a form of meditation, a different way of seeing, maybe even a kind of hallucination. Whenever I was with him I could tell when it was time to leave, but I never knew the direction we were headed for, or how long the walk would last. And most important, I never knew what our destination was. With him, everything was an adventure. Everything brought a new feeling.

In one occasion while traveling near the Uraba region where the banana plantations are located in Colombia, *we were on our way back from the jungle, loaded with the medicinal plants we had collected in the region. As we were walking along a street, we saw a lady who had a large wound in one leg. Cuatiendioy observed her calmly for a few seconds; then he laid down his belongings, went up to her and said, "Madam, I'm going to cure you of your ailment." The lady looked at us with indifference closely bordering on annoyance. This was understandable in view of our aspect. We stank with the dampness of the jungle.*

"Look here, sir," the lady replied. "If you can cure me, I'll pay you whatever price you ask. I've spent all my fortune trying to be cured from this acute ailment. I've been all over searching for doctors. I've visited the best clinics of this region. They've all told me they have no idea what's wrong with me. They say maybe it's an illness in my blood and that there is no cure for it."

Cuatiendioy wasn't listening to her. He was seeing something else. I was sure he attached no importance to her explanations. He kept looking at the lady's leg, which seemed as if it were afflicted with gangrene and alternately looking into her eyes, which were beginning to shine with a glimmer of hope.

"Madam, I need to go into your house," he said. "I want to have a look at all of the spaces there." Probably without understanding the reason for such an unusual request, the lady invited us into her house. Cuatiendioy went straight to her garden and sat down on a discarded tractor wheel. He took out a falcon feather from his bag, attached it to the middle finger nail of his left hand and began walking slowly, as if trying to keep the feather balancing on the finger. Then he stopped and told her, "Bring a shovel and dig right here." The lady looked clearly uneasy but she followed his instructions. She began to dig a hole and kept shoveling out dirt from it, until a small amber colored bottle appeared.

"Pick it up with your left hand," said Cuatiendioy, who was closely watching the lady. "We need to start a bonfire and burn it. Be very careful not to drop it. Under no circumstances can we risk breaking it before the fire is ready." We started the bonfire following Cuatiendioy's instructions. As soon as the fire was ready, he threw the bottle so violently at it that it smashed right in the middle of the flames.

"Madam, all you need to do now is to prepare a poultice with this herb and apply it on your wound. Keep the remainders in a small bag and hang it round your neck. Never take it off." The lady was speechless. She couldn't believe what had just happened. I quietly observed the whole scene while Cuatiendioy was gathering his things and getting ready to leave.

Some time later I was passing through that area again, and I took advantage of the occasion to pay this lady a visit. By that time, she had fully recovered her health. She told me about a woman who had coveted her husband some years before and had cast an evil spell on her to cause her husband to leave her. The curse was successful. When the ailment on her leg appeared, her husband left her. At the end of my visit, she begged me to ask Cuatiendioy how she could pay him.

When I told Cuatiendioy about my visit to this lady and her message about wanting to pay him, he asked, "Did you see that her leg was healed, Timoté?

"Yes, I did. It looks as if there had never been anything wrong with it."

Cuatiendioy said, "Then, if you happen to run into her again, tell her she has already paid me," and he walked on.

I had a hard time following him. I kept playing out the scene with the lady in my mind. I wanted to understand how someone could exert an influence on another person's body in that way. What was the source and the nature of that power to manipulate someone else's health? I was reflecting on these questions when Cuatiendioy interrupted me, "If you allow someone to enter into your space of energy and to steal your power, you're already dead, Timoté. No matter what trick the other person use. The measure of a man's strength depends on how far he is able to put his mind at his own service, and not be placed at the service of his mind. Become one with the jungle and let's move on. We've done enough talking today."

I followed close behind him, struggling to avoid thinking about the past. But past experiences kept appearing in flashbacks. In that context, the memory of another unexplainable encounter came to me.

Before our journey into the Amazon, I used to live in a small town where I first met Cuatiendioy. Our plan was to take a bus that went from the Pacific Ocean coast to the southern region. It was a thirty-six-hour bus ride to our point of destination. There we would be getting off and continuing on foot, on a trek that would take us deep into the Amazon jungle. The route the bus followed began in an area with beautiful landscapes, including plantations of bananas and other tropical fruits. At one point, the bus left the valley behind and climbed up the steep and craggy Andes mountains. The valley was out of sight at that point. The road became narrow and was literally smothered in vegetation. It felt as if one were going into a black hole from outer space, or a funnel that absorbed everything and kept it hidden for ten hours under the thick vegetation.

Just before this part of the road, there was a river that flowed at a leisurely pace. Its water was so clear that you could see the abundant wildife below: fish, turtles, snakes, and snails. It was the last point where travelers had a chance to stop and rest, drink some water, top up their radiators and take one last look at the valley.

From that point onwards, the road was narrow and dangerous. It was so poorly built that for several kilometers at a time, there was room for only one vehicle, so cars that were driving down had to stop for long stretches of time to leave space for the ones that were driving upwards.

In that exotic setting, I was to spend the afternoon with Cuatiendioy, who had purchased the bus tickets three days in advance. The bus service in that area was very limited. Their schedule included only two bus departures per day.

In addition to the hazards arising from the limitations of the precarious road, there was the recklessness of the bus drivers, who habitually drank large quantities of aguardiente (sugarcane spirits). This significantly contributed to making the journey even more dangerous than it already was. On that afternoon I shall never forget, there was a lot of people standing in line. We were in the vacations season, so people were waiting impatiently and anxiously to take the bus. Cuatiendioy looked them over calmly and said, "We're not leaving today. Go up to the counter and return our tickets." I couldn't understand his sudden decision. We had everything ready for the journey. Why should he postpone it? Of course I obeyed his intructions and took our tickets to the counter. Instantly they were bought by the next person in the line.

The bus was ready to leave, but its departure was being delayed because a man had gotten on the bus without a ticket and refused to give up his seat to the person who had the ticket precisely with that seat number. The man insisted that he would not get off the bus because he urgently needed to travel. He wanted to spend Christmas with his children. At the counter, he had been told there were no more tickets, but he had seen tickets being sold to other people who had been standing several places behind him in the line. He claimed there was preferential treatment for some "influential" customers.

The passenger who was the rightful occupant of that seat went to complain to the ticket office manager. In the meantime the driver, who was having a couple of drinks (blessings for the journey, as they called them) said: "You fight it out between yourselves. I'm late as it is!" And accelerating the ancient vehicle, he departed, leaving a cloud of dust behind him.

The man who had been claiming for his rightful seat on the bus was disappointed and furious. Across the street from the bus station, Cuatiendioy just sat meditatively, drinking a glass of water. I was upset because I had made plans to visit some friends and I was sure there wouldn't be any tickets until after Christmas.

The bus never reached its destination. That night, as it climbed up the steep slopes of the Andes, it was swept off a cliff by a huge landslide. There were no survivors. The man who lost his seat probably complained about his bad luck as he watched the bus driving away. I'm sure his complaint turned into gratitude when he heard the news of the tragic accident.

Just as everyone else, I was shocked by the news. Cuatiendioy didn't give me any explanation about his decision to return the tickets.

I kept trying to connect every past experience with some other event. But Cuatiendioy just said: "We won't make any progress this way. I can't be dragging you all the time. Become one with my stride. You'll get less tired and you'll move forward more swiftly. Stop ruminating on your thoughts like a cow. Look straight ahead." I softened my gaze. The swinging of Cuatiendioy's arms was barely perceptible. He moved with the rhythm of his arms and legs and seemed to be in a deep trance.

I followed him, treading wherever he would tread. Every obstacle revealed a solution that saved me from losing my rhythm. Walking in that state enabled me to see the jungle differently; it appeared different in its magic and in its colors. Walking was the ultimate peak experience. There was nothing else to do. The very notion that one could stop walking seemed absurd. I could walk around the whole world in this state but this time Cuatiendioy was the one who stopped.

He stopped right in front of an *higuerilla* bush and hugged it as if he were greeting a friend who was expecting him. I remained motionless, just watching him. He said, "Don't move." He walked in circles around the bush a few times, cut off some of its leaves, placed them under his arm, handed me some as well and instructed me to do the same. "Put them under your arm and on your hamstrings."

At that moment I suddenly began to feel my body. I thought I was going to pass out. I was aching all over. With my last remnants of strength, I did as he instructed and sat on my backpack.

"We'll be staying here today. This is a beautiful place, and it accepts us," he said joyfully.

My weariness went away instantly. I suppose it must have been the effect of the *higuerilla* leaves. We set about building a *temascal* to spend that night in. We lit the campfire and placed some stones in it which soon took on a reddish tint. Finally we opened our perception to the concert of the night.

Cuatiendioy curled up in fetal position and fell silent. It was the only time ever that I didn't see him sit in meditation before lying down to sleep.

The next day I woke up to the fragrance of tea. By that time, my sense of smell had become so highly developed that I could discern the presence of a squirrel. I could distinguish the smell of a deer's urine from a fox's or a wild dog's. I understood now why

Cuatiendioy would urinate every day on different spots, marking a circle as large as the space he felt we would need, and then telling me where to urinate. At first I was uncomfortable doing this, because I felt that by going so far as to regulate my urine he was exercising too much control over me, but I understood it now. No animal passed through that space without permission.

The day before had been very intense. We had covered a great distance in a state of completeness. I perceived the coldness of the jungle, the dampness of the *lianas* with the water dripping down from them, the sticky moss on my hands, the magic, the charm of walking in a different inner state. This was another space, a wide-open and luminous place. It was like a birthmark amidst the thick vegetation of the jungle, as if someone had cleared that space for a helicopter to land there. Or maybe Cuatiendioy had made it during one of his warming-up roamings. I valued those clearings in the middle of such thick foliage as a chance to feel the sun on my skin and to warm up my body with something else that wasn't tea or my imagination.

"We'll be staying a few days here. So let's make a worthy *temascal*, nice and warm. Don't forget to mark our space, Timoté,"

I set about marking the space immediately. In addition to it being warm, I felt it was the most beautiful spot in the whole jungle. I plunged into the construction of the *temascal* as if we were going to live there forever. We worked together, interweaving the leaves, and securing them with vine tendrils, much in the same way as if we were weaving a basket. Then we set up our indoor campfire in the middle of our beautiful dwelling. There was only room in it for us two, and even then provided we were sitting or lying down, so it was always warm. The smoke magically wafted its way out through a small opening we had left on the roof. So we could always heat up water for the tea, cook a few edible roots, pips or seeds and a bit of the bitter *yuko* fruit, which by then didn't taste so bitter to me. The tendril fastenings dried quickly. The *temascal* ended up having a fine structure and a different kind of magic.

"Tomorrow you'll begin to learn about some of the secrets of the jungle. I want you to become acquainted with the medicine of our ancestors. It's our greatest treasure. As you will see for yourself, it's all here."

I knew that. I had seen how Cuatiendioy could heal people. But I didn't think I could be interested in becoming a healer, because my father's expectations regarding my future were very different. At that point, I was only interested in getting out of the jungle. I wasn't afraid of the army any more, but I knew I wouldn't be able to find my way out of the jungle on my own. Besides my fear now had been transferred to the danger of falling into the hands of the guerrillas, who were always lurking in the areas surrounding small villages.

I remembered one day when we were exploring an area, trying to find a plant that would heal a farmer's kidneys, and we ran into a group of guerrillas among some bushes. They were waiting for nightfall so they could slip into town with one of their fighters who was sick and take him to see a doctor. The sick man complained so loudly of his pain that their hiding place was disclosed. When we went to the place the cries were coming from, the guerrillas jumped on us as soon as they saw us and immediately began interrogating us. When I explained that I was a fugitive from the army, they urged me to join their ranks. Fortunately, Cuatiendioy's intervention persuaded them to respect my freedom.

While I was telling them my story, Cuatiendioy prepared a paste made of herbs and placed it under the patient's nose so he could smell its scent. Based on where he pointed to when asked where he was feeling the pain, my impression was that he had appendicitis, After sedating him a bit with the herbs, Cuatiendioy started slowly stroking the right side of his belly, below the last rib, near his crotch. Then he began to rap on him sharply with his fingers, tracing an upward movement, as if he were trying to sweep up something that was inside, under the flesh. The man gave out a horrendous scream and his comrades instantly aimed their rifles at Cuatiendioy. He calmed them down saying, "That's it. Take him back with you and have him drink this tea."

Several days later we saw that man walking about the town, dressed in civilian clothes.

Although I was well aware of the depth of Cuatiendioy's knowledge of medicine, I had no interest in studying it. And I told him, "I'm not interested in knowing about herbs. I'm going to be an engineer."

"Poor Timoté. How you *do* get muddled up! You live not knowing what you are here for. You walk through life like a zombie, filling yourself up with stupidities. You will never achieve anything because you're always filling yourself with vain, ephemeral things, which in turn will bring you other similar things, which you call, and will continue to call, *"necessary."* You'll never achieve anything. You'll live to be an old man, possibly full of senseless possessions, consumed by fear, by sadness, afraid of losing all your things without ever having found the meaning of your existence. You'll die like *white men* do: full of everything, and without anything.

"At least allow me to heal your soul so that your departure may be more peaceful, so that you won't have to start out from the same point again, so that your children won't inherit your ignorance and they may be spared from repeating your mistakes. Those mistakes that are often the inheritance *white men* leave their children.

"Don't resist your instinct to break free from the ways of thinking you have always applied in the past. Otherwise you'll end up accepting that that is reality, that only *white men* are right because they've taken ownership of time. They've placed a restraint even on that. And they've placed a restraint on themselves as well. You mustn't fall into their trap because they will thwart your mind and your feeling. They'll suck you into their circle of power. They'll tell you: "This is your family, your people, this is your country, your fatherland, your continent, this is your religion and your truth. In this way, they will deprive you of your right to discover your own truth. To achieve their aim, they have a powerful weapon: distracting your mind with the game of "*things you need.*"

"Here you will learn about another medicine. No matter what you decide to be in the future, you won't be leaving this space with as much weight as you had when you came in. I must remind you that you're under the law of the *indio* and of the jungle here. With that sickness in your soul, you contaminate everything you touch and everything you see. If you're not interested in healing your soul, the jungle is interested in healing you because there is a power here, a purer energy. Fortunately for us, the *civilized man* has directed neither his eyes nor his thoughts towards this place yet. So there is nothing that is restrained here, nothing contaminated or measured. This is an ideal place for you to break free from your circle. So I'm going off to get some medicine that will heal your soul.

I noticed he was looking closely at a bird that moved restlessly among the trees. Cuatiendioy whistled at it several times, as if they were communicating with each other. I then realized I had seen that beautiful bird in every one of the places where we had been. Since it had happened in the jungle, I had assumed it was something normal, like so many other birds and their songs in that setting. But this time, I noticed that the bird replied to Cuatiendioy's whistling. After the bird flew away, I felt a burning curiosity regarding that bird's bond with Cuatiendioy; this man who sometimes seemed like a child and sometimes like a father, correcting my mistakes, or like a schoolmaster. On still other occasions, I saw him as a wise man who taught me about his life philosophy. Or a witch-doctor, who healed my fungal infections, and healed other patients. Right now he seemed to be a madman, talking to birds, searching for herbs to cure my soul. I couldn't understand his madness. How can you cure the soul with herbs?

Quite a while after he had gone off to search for the herbs, I heard the bird singing and then saw Cuatiendioy coming back from his expedition, carrying some orchids in a *guaje* and holding a thick bunch of leaves in his hands. He came up to me and pointing to the bunch of leaves said, "Look, Timoté. This is good medicine for weariness." Then showing me the beautiful orchids, he said, "These are to heal your soul. We'll leave them here until tomorrow. They'll work better after having been exposed to moonlight. Now we'll eat the last cornmeal buns and we'll drink this tea to relax our feet."

He warmed up two buns wrapped in green leaves and covered with cinders. He set the table as usual (a large green leaf over a dry log or a stone) and heated up the tea. We dined at the same leisurely pace as we always did, enjoying the taste of each morsel and visualizing that this food covered all our bodies' needs.

Cuatiendioy had taught me that the richness of food was in the richness of the spirit of the person who was eating it. He said that food becomes whatever the mind wants it to become and could be as abundant as I saw it, or as meager as I wanted it to be. My attitude could transform it into a medicine, or into a deadly poison. Actually those were the first teachings I received from Cuatiendioy before I went into the jungle with him.

The first time I ate *yuko*, I found that root so bitter that it turned my stomach and I refused to chew it. At the same time, my mind was full of doubts regarding how I should react. Cuatiendioy looked at me closely and said, "Timoté, that's no way to eat or drink anything, no matter what it may be. You're killing yourself, like all *white men* do. They eat with no respect for the food and no respect for their own health. Food becomes nourishment or poison, depending on your thoughts. *White men* make their food sick because their own souls are sick, and while they eat they are thinking about some revenge, or they are connected with their fears from the past or about the future, or they are thinking about their business, without paying any attention to their food. That's why it's so hard to heal a *civilized man*. Even when they take the medicine, they are connected with the grudge or the fear that generated their illness.

"This *yuko* will either be nourishment or it will kill you. For us *indios* it is a sacred food that has always protected us. It knows what to do in our bodies. We accept its bitter taste and the *yuko* accepts being our nourishment and our medicine. The *yuko* fruit accepted seeking for and processing from the soil everything that is good for the *indio*. The *yuko* sinks its deepest roots below and leaves some of them on the surface to capture the water and nourishment in the soil that doesn't go deep undergound; it captures the sun and transforms it. During the night, it is bathed by the moon and its magic so that the *indio* woman can also eat it. The *yuko* didn't know what it could do for the *indio* until the *indio* taught it. This took a long time, until the spirit of the *indio* and the spirit of the *yuko* were able to understand each other.

"So then, Timoté, here in the jungle you'll have to eat *yuko*, a rich and sacred food. Ask to be forgiven for the thoughts you had. Become one with it. You'll have to eat it with love. Otherwise it will become whatever you think it is. That's a covenant between the *yuko* and the *indio*, and you must remember that you are under our laws."

By that time, his teachings regarding food were clear to me. Now according to him, I was getting ready for the healing of my soul. So we started to eat the buns, while I imagined that I was eating some delicious Italian pasta and that the tea was a glass of excellent red wine. Likewise, the *temascal* was transformed into a cozy little house. I could also perceive the love with which that food had been prepared, and I could see a blue light springing out from it. I wasn't eating only a bun. What went into my mouth was light that was then transformed into energy, into life.

After we finished our meal, Cuatiendioy set about covering up holes in the texture of the *temascal*. He used leaves and tiny fibers. He was devoting a lot of effort to enhancing every detail of the construction. I saw this as a sign that we were going to stay here for a long time. Later in the deep darkness of the night, immersed in star constellations, and delighted with the concert offered by the crickets, my soul cut itself free from the *temascal* and entered into magical and unforgettable dreams.

VII

Encounter With The Orchids

The next morning, I woke up to the sound of Cuatiendioy's voice urging me to get up.

"Get up, Timoté. You've slept long enough."

I wasn't sure I wanted to get up. My head was spinning and I was sleepy. He, on the contrary, was as poised and calm as always.

"You won't be eating anything today. We'll begin to heal your soul and your past, so that that you'll be able to see the clues to your life more clearly. I hope you won't lose sight of your aim. Have a bit of this water and sit up." He handed me the *guaje*, with a beautiful orchid in it.

"Drink a bit of this, without damaging the orchid," he said.

He sat next to me. I had a few sips while I contemplated the orchid leaves, observing the beautiful colors beginning with a soft pink tone changing to a beautiful rainbow shade and ending with an intense red crimson. The orchid embodied all the colors of the jungle, colors that I was absorbing by drinking this precious water, bathing in light and color my whole body while observing the subtle petals floating in the humble *guaje*.

"Drink only a little bit," he insisted.

Then, touching my backbone, he asked me the usual question, "What do you see now?"

"*It's a warm morning. I'm up in the Andes. I live in a beautiful little village. The wind sways the pines and the willows. The clouds are low and thick. Below is the humble village. From this beautiful spot I can sometimes see its red-tiled roofs when the clouds float upwards and leave the vista free. There's a certain peacefulness about them. I have the impression of seeing my house floating over the clouds. Everything shines. We're happy, relaxed. I'm seeing my brother, who's urging me to go higher up with him to a peak with a clear view. He carries three books in his bag. We sit down by the river. My brother reads a book. I'm keeping him company.*

"*I'm watching the water. I hear the sound every drop makes as it crashes against the stones. I can feel the book. I'm enjoying its content, I feel it, I understand it. I haven't seen any of its pages, but I can perceive the feeling that emanates from my brother. My brother has completely become the book. My brother is afraid. His fear is with me. I can no longer perceive the clean, transparent water. We're both uneasy. I'm becoming the river, the water. The water has turned murky. We're both afraid. I feel I've lost control over my feet. I feel lost.*"

"All right. Come back. That's enough. I can see you started your life learning to fear, copying fears. Now you need to find new patterns. Just as you were able to become one with your brother while you were contemplating the river, and you were able to enter into the space of his thoughts, in the same way you can enter into other thoughts that are more positive and wiser. Why copy noises that are harmful to you? Seek for wise men, or allow yourself to be found by them. When you meet someone who awakens a feeling of admiration in you, set your mind free. Get near him and feel. You were imitating your brother. You sat just like he did and maybe you started breathing at his rhythm, helped by the soothing sounds of the water, and you stopped thinking. Feeling appears when there is absence of thought. And feeling is what's most important. From now on, try to feel more. Seek out people who have pleasant sensations and feelings and look into their eyes. A good man creates a healthy world. His thoughts spread all over and touch everything, even though they can't be seen. Thoughts cover everything, just like dust does. We *indios* leave our children with the grandparents so that they may pass on peacefulness and wisdom to them while we are out working in the fields.

"Now, drink some more of that same water. As you can see, it's orchid water. It has discharged its healing energy. I hope you have healed that experience. Also I want you to know that your brother has connected you with that book and with everything you are seeking for in the present."

"I don't know what I'm looking for, Cuatiendioy."

"What was the book about?"

"I can't remember. It was a book my father took special care of. He would keep it hidden amongst other books."

"I'm sure that book was important, Timoté. It must have contained information that was important for your father. That's why he had infused it with a different kind of energy, which in itself drew attention to it. That book had feeling."

He paused. "Go back to the book. Look at the book!"

"It's an old book. My mother doesn't like it very much. That's why my brother reads it on the sly. It's about alchemy and past lives. It's a weird book. My mother scolds my father for leaving those books in plain view, where my brother might see them."

"All right. Come back. You can understand the source of your uneasiness now. As you have seen, anyone who enters into a different kind of energy and feels it can never be the same again. Even if he tries to suppress his thoughts, he won't be able to suppress his feelings, because feelings settle on you in layers and cover every part of you, just like dust. So you can't see until you stop to examine the layer that is covering what you want to observe. Knowledge also settles on you and covers every part of you, like dust. Drink a bit more of this orchid water. It makes us aware of our fears. What did you decide at the time?"

"I don't know. I just remember the uneasiness that pervaded all my body, and from that moment onwards I felt the need to search for the unknown or whatever my father was so mysteriously searching for. I wanted to be a seeker, just like my brother. I enjoyed being near him. I wasn't a good reader but whenever he read something, I could feel his own curiosity within myself. I feel it's the same now. Whenever he talks about something he has experienced, I feel it myself. I feel within myself what he is saying."

"That's fine. It's a way to learn. But we'd better heal your soul so you'll never forget what you've learned. I want you to see the orchids, to *feel* them, to listen to everything. You'll see how effective they are. They are the best remedy for healing the soul."

"How will I know when I'm cured?"

"Forget about your mind. Always follow your heart. Become one with every moment; become one with everything. We need to continue with your healing. I need you to come with me so we can both ask the jungle for permission together, since we're going to take from it something that is the most fragile and the most beautiful, just for your healing. Follow me, and bring your *guaje* along."

I followed him with a bit of apprehension regarding this new healing session. The previous sessions had been so painful that I wasn't sure I wanted to continue with these strange practices. On the other hand, my first experience with the orchid seemed to indicate that this time the healing method would be gentler.

We walked until we came to an area near the swamp. It was hard to walk there. As soon as he set one foot on the ground, Cuatiendioy would instantly raise the other one. He seemed to float on the boggy soil. My boots were steeped in mud. I was having a hard time trying to coordinate the movements of my feet through the mud without sinking into it. Judging by the tracks in the surrounding area, it was clearly a watering place for a large number of wild animals. There were many orchids all around, which brightened the spot with an array of beautiful colors. Some of the orchids hanging from the branches gave the impression of

floating or dancing over the swamps. Every tree in the process
of dying was resurrected through the colors of the beautiful and
exotic orchids. This multicolored garden gave the impression of
being harvested by a special being. Fluttering over them were
thousands of butterflies, and a vast variety of insects displaying an
unimaginable range of hues and tints. I imagined how a painter
or a photographer would love to capture the beauty of this scene.

Cuatiendioy bowed to them, as if he were greeting a friend
and said, "Notice how such beautiful flowers grow in the midst
of swamps. We'll find a suitable place where we can sit down.
Some spot that is drier."

He picked a few aromatic twigs, rubbed them between his
hands, and offered me some as well. We rubbed our bodies with
our hands and the mosquitoes instantly went away.

"Sit up properly. It's time for you to understand that each plant
or flower brings its own beneficial effect. Today we're going to
center our attention and our energy on orchids, because they are
the ones that heal the soul. There are many doctors who can heal
the body, Timoté. Healing the body is easy but the *civilized man*
likes to make it difficult. If he understood that when you heal
the soul, you are also healing physical ailments, there wouldn't
be so much sorrow in the world. There wouldn't be so many
sick people. The soil would be healthier; there would be more
respect for life and for the jungle. Orchids will become good
allies for you. Human beings can commune with them in the
contemplation of their delicate colors. Color is the densest part
of an orchid.

"The *civilized man* grasps the orchid's color but the *indio* grasps
its spirit. The spirit hides *behind* the color. This is beyond the
civilized man's understanding. He can't understand how an orchid's
fragrance can heal his soul. His sense of smell is not subtle enough
for this. Since he is not capable of communing with orchids
because of all the noises he carries in his mind, he needs to cut
them off and take them with him to decorate his meaningless

external spaces. When his soul is sick and he comes near a flower, the flower calls to him, whispers at him but he can't hear it. He's lost in the midst of his noises and his haste. That's why he dies without ever having understood that the reason for his death is to be found in his soul.

"The *civilized man* seeks outside and forgets about the inside. His pride grows whenever he punishes himself. And pride kills. Disharmony kills. *White men* spend most of their time hoarding. They want to appropriate and hoard everything they see. Everyone covets everyone else's possessions. Whatever they build always seems to be based on destruction. They're never satisfied. You know why? Because the *civilized man* is estranged from the spirit of the earth and has placed his heaven and his gods very far away. His gods are so high up and far away that they can't see how their children kill one another in their struggle to reach those same gods whose kingdoms they have never understood and will never understand.

"This is so, because the *white men's* selfish yearnings are aimed at living eternally in a state of happiness that they have never found in this heaven that is life, this beautiful paradise, our beloved earth. That's why the gods of the *indios* weep. They also weep because of the *civilized man's* ignorance. Watch, the water is weeping. Isn't the God of Water the same god the *civilized man* prays to and whose return under the form of rain he begs for, whenever a town is left without water for a few days? The God of Water is in the water of the orchid, of the *yuko* and of the *liana*. The *indio* finds the God of Water in the spirit of everything. The *indio* finds the God of the Sun in the spirit of the sun. God peeks down on us every morning with the sun, and the indio greets the God of the Sun.

"The *indio* feels the God of the Wind in the evening winds. And if He doesn't come in the evening, he waits for the the God of the Wind during the night. But he knows He will come, and there is no anxiety in the *indio* if the wind delays its arrival, because He will come more strongly after His silence. The God of the Wind will not cease bringing coolness to the huts of the *indios*; that's why the *indio* dances for the spirit of the wind. The *indio's* God is strong and does not expect to be defended by the *indio*; he defends Himself on his own. He will defend Himself from the *civilized man* punishing him from afar. Or He will arrive with such force that He will teach the *civilized man* to respect the Earth.

"The *civilized man* hasn't been able to understand his Gods, who are so far away. That's why the earth hasn't been able to reveal its secrets to the *white men*. There's no one to communicate with. Today we'll start with the spirit of the flowers. They are what comes first. We need to heal the *civilized man* with the flowers. We need to teach him to love them, to use them, to feel them, and to look after them. Go out there, wherever you like, fetch an orchid and bring it here. Don't forget to ask permission from the spirit of the orchid."

I went over to an ancient tree. On its moss-covered trunk, there were about ten orchids. I approached it cautiously and pulled off a blue and red orchid, taking care not to damage its roots. I walked back to Cuatiendioy, who had kept his eyes on me all the time.

He finally spoke, "Fix your gaze on it without focusing. I want you to see beyond its shapes, beyond its color. Observe the orchid's energy. You can ask it any question. But you mustn't listen for the answer on the outside. Listen on the inside. Become one with the orchid. Ultimately, we are all the same spirit. The spirit that moves the orchid is the same spirit that moves you and me. Transform yourself into the orchid. Become one with it! Sit down with your gaze straight ahead of you. Hold the orchid in your left hand. Don't think of anything and perceive it. Start by feeling it. Touch its petals without damaging them. The orchid is as delicate as the iris of your eyes. Sense its roots, attached to that olive green stem. It has always depended on that tiny stem. Now it depends on you. Make it feel your love so that it may shine. Convey a noble feeling to it, and watch how it changes."

I didn't know whether it was Cuatiendioy's words that made me see so much beauty or whether it was all real, but I felt immersed in that subtle beauty.

He picked up a twig, pulled off its leaves and held it close to my eyes. "Keep your eyes on it. I'm going to take you to a different state of consciousness, to the consciousness of flowers."

I followed the movement of the twig, keeping my gaze fixed on it all the time. I could feel Cuatiendioy's movements along with the sensation of layers being peeled off my eyes. Then he touched my forehead with his forefinger and said, "That's it! Keep your eyes still now!"

Then he walked away a few yards and sat down on the ground. He adopted the lotus position and fell silent.

My eyes were motionless. I felt as if they were tightly shut, but I was seeing the orchid and all the other orchids around me. I felt my head was a huge eye and my whole body an enormous ear. My senses were completely open and perceptive.

Cuatiendioy remained sitting in deep silence, anchored to the earth. I could hear his breathing although he was sitting at some distance from me. I went into his rhythm. I felt the orchid I held in my hand joining us both in our rhythm. The soil was breathing. It was alive, just like the orchids. Each one of them had one inner color and six outer colors. The colors had movement. Without letting go of my orchid, I directed my attention to other orchids that caught my interest. I perceived something more than their beauty. I experienced indescribable feelings, complete oneness; the orchid was part of me, or we were both one and the same thing. We clung with our roots to the bark of the tree trunk and our fragrance permeated the jungle. I felt I was in paradise again. I was the tree, the rock, the fragility of the orchid. I was everything.

Cuatiendioy and I were motionless, so much so that two deer that passed very near us totally ignored us. We seemed like two ghosts of the jungle. Two ghosts who existed without time, without space, without shapes, intertwined in one rhythm. One silent and harmonious rhythm.

It was late when Cuatiendioy returned to his body and said, "Stop your mind and the world stops. If there are no noises inside your mind, not even animals can perceive your existence. It's time to leave. That's all for today."

Regaining control over my body was extremely painful for me. My knees ached terribly and my legs were numb. But the experience I had just had was worth whatever pain I had to suffer.

We walked back to the *temascal* without uttering a single word. We ate some tiny bananas and lit the campfire. There was nothing I wanted to ask. All questions felt redundant. Cuatiendioy made tea and invited me to sit next to him. The warmth his body radiated was intense and pleasant. His body gave off a characteristic scent that I could recognize at a distance.

"Well, Timoté, I like it here. Look in front of you, among the trees. There comes the spirit of the moon. Would you like to meet her? Let's start a bonfire to present our greetings to the moon and to allow the moon to let us see her spirit. I want you to see, feel and touch the spirits that accompany the world of the *indio*, but it will not become your own reality unless you experience it inside yourself."

We set about collecting twigs and logs. When we had the amount we needed, Cuatiendioy said, "Let's put the logs leaning against each other, as in an embrace, and standing upright. That's how trees die. Facing up to the sky, they will give up their lives to the spirit of the moon. It would be an insult to have them die lying down, as if they were sick."

Following his instructions, I brought a burning log from the *temascal*, and used it to get the fire started. After briefly stoking it, we had a full bonfire going.

"We'll dance to the moon and pray for the earth," Cuatiendioy said and sat down to contemplate the fire, instructing me to sit facing him, on the opposite side of the bonfire.

When the moon was directly above our heads, Cuatiendioy said, "It's time for us to talk with the moon. Come nearer. We'll dance on the left."

He walked over to the *temascal* and came back with a *guaje*. He started beating on it rhythmically with a small stick. We followed the rhythm chanting, "*hueeeja, hueeejaiona..., hueeeja, hueeeja.iona, huejaiona hay hayhay...*" and stomped on the ground as we danced.

With the dance, the bonfire, the moon and the *guaje* drum, I went into a trance and remained hypnotized for the rest of the night. I sat in front of the bonfire, bathed in moonlight. Cuatiendioy did the same, sitting in his customary lotus position.

The moon was right above our heads. Its beams caressed the trees with a bluish tint that was very different from the one I was used to seeing. It was a light that reached all the way down to the roots of the enormous *ceibas*, creating the impression that they were the ones that held the earth between their huge tentacles, traveling at fantastic speeds across those skies full of delicately shy stars.

Multi-colored lights drifted up from the earth to the moon, phosphorescent vapors that soared far beyond the limits allowed by the force of gravity. I looked at Cuatiendioy and was dazzled by the shining halo around his head, which extended down to his feet and formed a plume of bright white light.

I watched him with amazement, as different layers of color began appearing, covering his body. The white plume acquired an intense reddish tint, and Cuatiendioy disappeared amidst a cloud of colors, leaving an incandescent silhouette, which seemed to be melting into the bonfire. As the inner reddish tints faded away, Cuatiendioy blended into the darkness, which was not complete due to the brightness of the moon. Then new shapes appeared. There was a new silhouette of outer colors and I saw that, in the empty space within, Cuatiendioy was no longer there. I could neither see him nor feel him. All that was left of him were his layers of light. I had the impression that he had disappeared before my very eyes. I was afraid I would lose him forever, but my perception changed instantly. I made contact with my body and with that other reality.

My heart was beating fast; I could feel that the energy of the moon had penetrated every single cell of my body, and that this energy urged me to keep on dancing. At the same time, I felt everything was moving. I was the dance, the Earth, the moon, the sun and the stars. I could feel no distance with the infinite. The universe could fit in my body or my body in the universe. We were one and the same thing. It was the totality, and it was nothingness.

In this suspended state, I had no notion of what was fantasy and what was reality. There was neither time nor space. There was neither above nor below. Shapes disappeared. I tried to move but I couldn't. My whole body was paralyzed, and so flabby that it seemed to be floating in a gelatinous mass. The moon had disappeared, and we were there, spent and motionless, facing the magic of a new day.

I found myself lying on the ground. Cuatiendioy was sitting, with his eyes half-closed, in a state of contemplation. I stood up. I was freezing. I went over to the *temascal* to prepare something hot to drink, accompanied by the morning song of the jungle.

Ever since that time, whenever there is a full moon, I think of Cuatiendioy. I imagine him singing in the Amazon jungle, *"hueja, huejahionahuejahuejaiona,"* and I yearn to float in infinite space once again.

Cuatiendioy soon joined me and said, "Lie down for a while. We've had an excess of exposure to the spirit of the moon. Get some rest. Sleep. We'll continue with your healing later."

I obeyed Cuatiendioy's instructions and lay down. With the warmth of the *temascal*, I soon fell into a deep sleep. I don't know how long I slept because when I woke up I had the impression that I had fallen asleep only a few seconds before. The difference was that I felt my energies fully replenished. I was ready to set out with Cuatiendioy immediately and walk for as many days as may be required.

Cuatiendioy had been waiting for me to wake up so that we could have breakfast together. He had prepared roasted *chontaduro* palm fruit and *boldo* tea, which was an unusual combination compared to the meals we habitually took.

Once we had finished having our breakfast, he said, "From now on, you'll only be drinking orchid water. We have enough of it to heal your soul. First, we're going to look for the *guajes* we need for the potions. And, while we're at it, we'll collect some fruit and seeds. But we won't be eating any *yuko* for now."

He stood up and, as usual, whistled several times. Instantly, a bird alighted on an enormous tree in response to Cuatiendioy's summons. It was his ally, the one that had always been present since we first came into the jungle. Also as usual, Cuatiendioy walked in a circle, following the sounds made by the bird. There was mutual communication between them and also between Cuatiendioy, the bird, and the forest. No matter what Cuatiendioy was seeking for, he was always able to find it so easily that he seemed to be just fetching something he himself had stored, planted or hidden, for example, the creepers full of wild pumpkin gourds that were right before my eyes.

He instructed me to pick the drier ones. He collected some of the greener ones and extracted their juice and seeds. We tied them together and made a nice and sizable bunch.Then, Cuatiendioy said, "Take them to the *temascal*. I'l be back soon."

I went back to the *temascal* to clean out the *guajes* and to extract the few remaining seeds that were still in them. Then I took them to rinse out in the pond where I had been the day before. It was the same spot where orchids grew nearby. I sat on my haunches and set about rinsing the *guajes* and while I did so, I contemplated the orchids. They were still beautiful but not as beautiful as they had been the previous day. I heard the bird singing and its presence triggered a connection with Cuatiendioy in my mind. I felt glad realizing that there were three of us now, and it had always been so, although my failure to become one with them had prevented my noticing it.

Cuatiendioy arrived with some fruit I had never seen before, a cluster of small berries that oozed a sweet, sticky liquid. He also brought roots, bananas and seeds. We ate to our hearts' content.

We filled the *guajes* with water and placed a different orchid in each one of them. Then we took them to the *temascal*. Cuatiendioy made a cut in a stalk similar to an aloe plant and added a drop of its liquid to each *guaje*. He said, "We'll let them rest. Each one will need some time to deposit its energy. Come nearer, observe, try to just see them, without comparing them. Stop in front of the one that calls your attention more powerfully."

The orchids were in the *guajes,* with fresh water from the stream. They were all beautiful, but only one of them captured my attention. Its glow was different. Its color was intense.

"That one!" he said. "Bring that one. It's the one we'll start with. Watch it closely." While I observed the orchid, he was observing me.

The *guajes* with the flowers in them had been on hold for several days. So had I. Cuatiendioy remained as calm as if he had all the time in the world. After a few days like this, I woke up feeling sad one morning. I felt I had been in the jungle long enough and was tired of contemplating the orchid. I wanted to see other people and be able to talk with them. I felt irritable and uneasy. I couldn't conceal my negativity any longer. I was restless and unhappy. Cuatiendioy just observed me calmly and finally said, "It's time to start with the flowers. For the next few days, you'll only drink this orchid's water. Be sure not to mix it with water from the other orchids. It wouldn't be good for your healing process."

"What healing process are you talking about? There's nothing wrong with me. I don't even have the slightest pain."

"I'm talking about your soul, Timoté. Just drink from this *guaje*. You'll need to find your calmness to become one with the best part of you and with the jungle again."

"All right. I'll drink that water," And I did. It was colorless, unlike the water from the *lianas* we had drunk on other occasions.

"Fine, Timoté. Drink some more. Take small sips, and swallow slowly. Only three times a day. Surrender yourself to the orchid every time you want to contemplate its beauty. Be careful not to damage it. If you see the amount of water in the *guaje* is diminishing, add more water to it before it dries up."

I cupped my hands, poured a little water onto them and took a small sip. It tasted like damp jungle and had the fragrance of moss. I drank from that *guaje* for three days. I felt comfortable and open to whatever instructions Cuatiendioy might give me. For his part, he kept strolling calmly around the *temascal* and observing me constantly.

During that week I had nothing to drink but orchid water. My dreams became more vivid. There was a transparent beauty in all things. I paid special attention to taking care of my body. There was a harmonious rhythm in the water of the stream. Bathing in it was like a ritual for me. I felt I was leaving behind all my feelings of guilt and all of my negativity. What I ate was no longer important to me. What mattered were the contents within the shapes. A banana contained a beauty that was prior to its taste. The *yuko*, that root I had often hated to eat, had a purple-blue tinted energy that made me eager to chew on it, although I wasn't allowed to eat it just then. The bird that kept us company was not just another bird. It was a new friend who spoke to us about the jungle with its singing.

Drinking the orchid water was helping me to change my way of seeing life. I wanted to keep on drinking that wondrous water but at one point, Cuatiendioy told me I had had enough. I only say "at one point" because I had lost all track of days and dates. They just didn't fit in with this experience. Time didn't matter and there was no reason at all to hurry for anything. There was nothing to distinguish one day from another except for the delight of a new bird, the offspring in a hummingbird's nest, a doe with its fawn, a raccoon, a sloth, or an insect I had never seen before. Days and dates had already become irrelevant as from my first days in the jungle. Just as my notes had. At first, they had been important to me. Later on, every detail would become engraved in my soul. Whenever I wanted to recall something, all I needed to do was close my eyes and I would remember the slightest details. Even fragrances. The word "scientific" became totally unimportant, as did my compass, my papers and my pens.

"Stop drinking that water. You mustn't grow too fond of the orchid. You can become addicted to it. You'd better continue with this other one."

He handed me a *guaje* with a new orchid and urged me to drink from it. I didn't like the change at all. I was thoroughly happy with the one I had. So while I reluctantly changed orchids, I asked him how much longer we were going to remain there. "A few days. About three more orchids. Right now, the time is up to them. The orchids will be your clock. Each one of them will show you the time according to your sickness."

"What sickness? I'm not sick at all.

"You sickness is in your soul, Timoté. Anyone with healthy eyes can see it. Now stop asking questions and drink up your water."

I drank from the new water, but there was no difference in its taste. A few hours later, I began to feel restless. I wanted to go deeper into the forest, leave everything behind, walk to any place whatever. I went up to Cuatiendioy and told him, "I want to go gather some firewood, an amount large enough to make a bonfire."

"All right, I'll come with you."

"I'm going alone," I remarked with annoyance. "I was on my own for nine days and now you tell me I need you to go with me to gather some firewood? Do you think I'm a child?"

"All right, go alone. But if you feel scared for any reason, trace a circle of power and get inside it. Wait there until I come to get you or until you've recovered your strength."

I went deeper into the jungle by myself. something inside me needed to alone, so I decided to find my "own" unique silence within the jungle, and then I was caught by an overwhelming feeling of restlessness. I saw a cloud of insects flying about that drove me away from the temascal. I felt desperate and thought I heard the plants speaking to me. I knew where the wild boar was, the deer, the raccoon, the jaguar, any living creature of the jungle. I could smell each one and distinguish them from one another without the slightest possibility of error. I also knew Cuatiendioy was nearby. I caught sight of him observing me from behind a leafy myrtle tree, and shouted at him, "What do you want, Cuatiendioy?"

"Nothing. You're out of your mind. This is the Amazon. If you keep walking in that direction, you'll sink into the swamp. It's not your time yet to be devoured by crocodiles. Go back and become one with the orchid."

I went back, feeling upset. The whole place was annoying to me. Nothing seemed to cheer me up. When we got to the *temascal,* I sat down and Cuatiendioy immediately traced a circle around me with some branches. I lost all my strength and was unable to stand up.

Memories from my childhood started coming to me. They were all related to the issue of time management: "It's the time for your bath…time to go to school… time to bring the cows in… time for lunch…time for dinner…time to pray.. time to go to bed… time to sleep… it's time, it's time, it's time…look at your watch, it's late already, it's very late, it's early, there's no time for… it's already time for… time, a lot of time, little time, no more time, when there is time, if I had time…"

I felt deeply troubled. Each memory worsened the churning in my stomach. I felt there was a ball that kept growing inside me and was out of control. The dialogues about time wouldn't stop. My anguish grew in the same measure as the ball in my stomach grew. I had the same feeling I used to experience when I was a child, when the idea of time would creep into the best moments of my childhood games and spoil them, or when in the midst of deep contemplation of a star I would hear a voice that said, "Time is up, it's time to go to bed now," and my feeling of awe would become frustration, and frustration would fuel the growth of the ball in my stomach.

Every memory related to time became clearer and with them, I vividly experienced all over again the feelings lodged in my stomach. Now the ball had grown so large that it began to make it difficult for me to breathe. I wanted to run, but I couldn't even stand up. I shouted, "Help me, Cuatiendioy!"

"What's the matter?"

"Time is killing me!"

"Don't let it."

"How do I do that?"

"That's your problem."

"Time is choking me to death!"

"You can do it! Don't let time defeat you!"

"And how can I defeat time?"

"Let go of it!"

"I can't"

"Then die with it!"

The sensation of the ball grew so much that I lost my voice, and I thought I was going to die. At the same time, all my memories of time-related anguish appeared to me as vividly as if they were happening in the present. The process in my stomach became more intense and spread to all my organs. A deafening noise came out of my throat. I vomited a green, bitter, sticky substance. After that I lay on the ground, huddled up and hugging my stomach.

"You vomited your time anguish. What a strange way *white men* have with time. They live tangled up with time and they die at the wrong time."

When I was able to stand up, I felt light and calm, as if it had all been only a dream or a nightmare. However, as evidence that it had been real, I still had the green mixture I had thrown up and the bitter taste that lingered in my mouth.

"You're already lighter, Timoté. You got rid of a lot of weight. That's good for your journey. Now give thanks to the orchid, and remember you are the one who owns time."

I went to the *temascal* and prepared some tea to get rid of the bitter taste in my mouth. The taste gradually went away as the memories of all my conflicts with time also faded away. The sensation lasted until the following day.

I described to Cuatiendioy everything I had felt.

"It's the *civilized man's* foremost sickness. With it, they contaminate everything. And the worst part of it is that they lose the gift of hearing, seeing and feeling." Cuatiendioy adopted one of his ironical moods. "But don't worry. It's "only" a sickness of the soul. It brings a different kind of pain. It "only" hurts mostly on the day of your death. Before that, there's no time to see it, to feel it and to discover it.'

Reverting to his usual tone, he continued, "You need to be able to recognize this illness and avoid it. It's very easy to be infected by it, as easy as becoming addicted to smoking. That's how *white men* live, running after time, they barely have any time. What for? Or, why? In the end, time carries them away, and they have no idea where to. Now, just give thanks to the orchid and get ready for the next one."

I spent a relaxed afternoon, while I reflected on what time had meant to me and the anguish I had experienced whenever I felt I wouldn't have enough time to do things I considered important. That night I slept peacefully. When I woke up the next day, Cuatiendioy was waiting with the morning dose ready for me. He suggested that this one would work better in helping me to avoid being afraid of the orchids.

"Drink this one now. It'll be better for both of us."

It was a gorgeous orchid, with remarkable colors, pink and white with red and violet tips.

"This one is friendlier, and although it only has an effect on part of you, it'll be quite useful. It's better this way. Your living friends from the jungle will be able to recognize you. When you become one with all of them, they will also become one with you."

I couldn't deny that I was happy in that moment. I accepted all, and felt that I was accepted by all.

Several weeks went by while we changed orchids. Knowing what each orchid could do no longer mattered to me. I knew that Cuatiendioy was giving me what he considered adequate for my healing process. Each one of them fulfilled its function, making connections with different events from my past. Traumatic experiences were cleared up, serious ones as well as minor ones, and Cuatiendioy would help me break free from them, having me drink water from the orchid he considered adequate for my healing.

One day, while I was drinking water from an orchid he had selected, I was leaning forward, my gaze lost in the deep greenness of the jungle. I couldn't let go of a branch I was clutching tightly and I had a lump in my throat. I had the sensation of carrying a lead weight on my back. I had feelings of deep sorrow, coupled with anger and frustration. Cuatiendioy, who was watching me, perceived what I was going through. He approached me and helped me let go of the branch and said, "All right, it's time for you to let the anger out. Hit on whatever you want to."

And handing me a stick, he said, "Just hit once and for all. Say what you feel. Say it, Timoté."

I leaped up instantly and began to hit everything that stood in my way. I yelled like a savage and wept like a child. Meanwhile, Cuatiendioy kept shouting: "That's it, Timoté! Finish that one off! Hit hard, Timoté! Harder! Curse him and finish him off! This is the time to let out your anger!"

I felt my anger and kept on hitting until my strength was gone. I destroyed everything that stood in my way. I smashed the stick to smithereens. Then I sat down and wept, overcome with sorrow and frustration.

Cuatiendioy drew close and spoke into my ear, "Weep and hit, but you need to know who you are hitting, and why you are weeping. Don't budge now. Just get in touch with it and say what you are feeling."

I felt I was beating up the army, the guerrillas, my own frustration and all those who were guilty of the death of my friend, Fabio. *He was friendly with everyone in the neighborhood. A great soccer player, with the energy of a gazelle and with the gift of inspiring laughter and joy in anyone who came near him. He was the eldest son in a family of peasant migrants who sought refuge in the city, having fled from the horror of the war with the guerrillas. Overcoming all the difficulties of adapting to city life, his father found a job in a cookie factory and his mother baked pastries to sell in order to ensure that their three children should have an education. Fabio was the smartest of the family, and was always finding ways to get ahead. He ran errands for neighbors, sold newspapers, and was always on the lookout for a chance to earn a few coins.*

Anyone who needed something urgently, for example some medicine from the pharmacy, could rely on him. Besides, he had purchased a soccer ball with his savings. This placed him in a position of privilege amongst the youths of the neighborhood. As the owner of the ball, he decided who could be on the teams. I was thankful to Fabio because he always picked me even though, frankly, I wasn't a good player and most of the time I just ran after the ball, getting in the way of my fellow team members. They all laughed at my lack of skills but Fabio would tell me during soccer games, "You just go and make it difficult for the other team to advance." Fabio was my friend and a friend to everyone in the neighborhood.

One morning, the streets were flooded with army green uniforms. Armored cars and war tanks sprang up from every direction. Everyone locked their doors, but there were still some people out in the streets. They were inspected, one by one. The soldiers knocked on every door and if someone didn't open their door, they knocked it down.

In that time, there were some magazines in circulation that contained communist propaganda. They were quite popular because of discontent and violence caused by the politicians in power and their families, who took turns handing over the government to one another. So the rest of the population would look for a solution to this, whatever it may be.

Those who were most strongly opposed to the government took up arms and joined the fight against the regime. My friend Fabio and I were students, and we were against the government. For that reason, we sometimes took part in demostrations and protest marches in the streets. We used to chant, "The People, united, shall never be defeated!"

Our aim in participating was to try to help make the echoes of the protest grow, so that somewhere in the world someone would listen to us, because our rulers were deaf and blind. I must admit they were very skillful in terms of making speeches full of lies, just like all Latin American politicians. At this point, they had only one argument: violence, and that morning they wanted to prove it once more.

I was watching the disgusting spectacle from the rooftop of my house, on a third floor, when I saw Fabio coming out of the pharmacy with his first errand of the day. The soldiers assaulted him, beat him up, threw him up into the air and onto a truck full of soldiers who brutally started kicking him,

I still remember the expression of terror in Fabio's eyes, when he tried to catch the bottle of cough syrup that flew up into the air and was smashed when it fell on the ground. Señora María, one of the neighbors, cried out, "Fabio, the cough syrup! No, it's not possible!"

Señora María had been waiting for Fabio to bring a bottle of cough syrup for her son. She went out to try to reason with the soldiers, but all her arguments and pleadings were in vain.

Fabio walked by, bleeding, right before my eyes. Horrified, I saw him being taken, along with several other youths of my neighborhood. We all waited for news of Fabio. His parents and friends made every effort possible to get him back but the army considered him a revolutionary and forcefully recruited him. They cared nothing about the interruption of his education. He was recruited to go out and kill revolutionaries.

From the city, we followed the news of clashes between rebels or guerrillas and the army. By then, Fabio had become an enemy of the people. He was forced to take part in combats and wherever he marched through, he was hated. He wrote a letter to his parents, narrating his experiences in the war and saying that he was trying to learn how to be a car mechanic, to get excused from combat duty. He explained how he tried to be obient, to avoid being sent to massacres.

One day, a black butterfly alighted on the door of Fabio's room in his parents' home. That afternoon, an army truck arrived with a black coffin, which contained Fabio's corpse. Later during the funeral, an officer wearing his gala uniform, made the other "Fabios" stand in line. After much weepling, the neighborhood fell silent.

"Fabio," said the army officer, as he delivered the coffin to his parents, "has died for our country. You must be proud of him."

They covered him with the flag and set up a guard of honor, with some soldiers that stood as rigid as statues. That day I forged my anger, my frustration, my sadness. I looked at my friend's lifeless body and asked myself how far the echoes of our shouting in the square had traveled. That day, I made the decision that I would never serve in the army. I found an outlet for my anger in writing this poem.

> That symbol of horror
> that marches up the streets.
> That symbol of horror
> that marches down the streets.
> That murky green
> that invades transparent spaces,
> that leers out of the corner of its eye,
> that marches forward with an upright posture,
> that gives a terrifying, peculiar ring
> to the order of 'Halt!'
> That symbol of death

gazes forward.
Under the black boot
crushed thoughts,
dead poets,
dead writers,
dead audiences.
The street of History,
a river of stories,
shall be a symbol of horror.
Of symbols I speak.
The ascending street,
the descending street.

That symbol of horror that marches up the streets, that symbol of horror that marches down the street: my feeling was so deeply buried within me that I was barely aware of the significance of the rifle slung over my shoulder. No struggle made sense any longer if it was based on violence. I had just let out all my repressed violence, as well as all my frustrated feelings.

In this corner of the Amazon, with this soul mate, I was letting out all that anger, the anguish, the frustration. Hitting with that stick, I was lashing out at the rulers who were then in power and at my own frustration.

I had never agreed with war or with any kind of violence. War brings on war, blood attracts blood. But that day, I realized I had violence within me, and even if I had done a large amount of thrashing, I didn't believe the government had suffered the slightest pain.

I told Cuatiendioy the story of my friend, Fabio. He listened with the patience of a father, or of a sage. When I finished telling my story, he said, "Timoté, that was nothing. For what's in store for us, you'll need to steel your soul. The future will bring even more bloodshed. But it too will pass. This earth will descend until it comes to know what hell is. Then you'll remember this.

You'll know when. This is only the beginning. As long as the changes made by *white men* are aimed only at obtaining money and power, there will be no changes. We *indios* have equitable rulers. You won't find any wealth in a *Curaca*, because the only thing he accumulates is knowledge of the earth and of the jungle. One day, *white men* will have to return to the Curacas. *White men* are sick. All of them are. Their sickness comes from the soul.

My body was aching all over, but I had a feeling of inner peace.

"Give thanks to the orchid. Forgive your past. Leave behind your fear of the army. If you've already made the decision of not going to war, then you won't go. Put put an end to your inner war. If you had been in the army, you would have completed your tour of duty already. Look at you! In your mind you are still wearing those boots and with the rifle slung over your shoulder. Do you think I don't feel it? With all that noise you carry around, it would take just one look at you for any soldier to know you're a fugitive. Your whole body is screaming it. From now on, you'll become another person. Leave your fear of the army behind. You won't go with them. I promise you."

With these words of reassurance, I went down to the stream. As I dived into the water, I left behind forever all of my negative thoughts and all of my fear of the army. On a later occasion, I was able to verify this. *We had left the jungle and came across army units that were conducting raids in search of guerrilla fighters and army deserters. I was walking side by side with Cuatiendioy at a bus terminal. We were traveling to the northern region of the country. Every passenger was being frisked and had to show identification documents. One by one, they would walk in front of the soldiers, who selected those who would be either the next victims or the next forced recruits. Cuatiendioy stood still for a few seconds and said, "Timoté, send all your weight downwards. Imagine there's nothing in your upper part. There's nothing in your head. Don't think. Let your feet take you. Fix your gaze on my back and follow me." He moved forward through the lines as if he were a commander who overrode anyone who stood in his way. He also seemed to hypnotize everybody, including me, as I walked behind him. He walked on as if he were oblivious to everything around him. He ignored the soldiers as he walked right past them. He climbed on the bus, and ignored the driver as well. We found seats in one of the middle rows of the bus and sat down.*

Completely unaware of what had just happened, the soldiers carried on with their routine. I saw how several youths about my age were pulled out of the lines and placed under surveillance as they clutched their few belongings. They would be future soldiers, or future victims. In other words, other "Fabios."

Many years later, I had a similar experience in Venezuela, which, at that time, was a prosperous country, due to the wealth derived from their abundant oil reserves. Many individuals from neighboring countries wanted to find work there, so there were strict controls on immigration at the border.

Venezuela was very strict regarding identification documents. No travelers by land, sea or air were allowed in without duly presenting their documents at airports, checkpoints or customs offices. I had embarked on a journey of adventure. I wanted to know the Orinoco, the Great Savannah and the highest waterfall in the world. By that time, I had obtained a certificate of military service compliance. It had been a difficult process, but I finally had it, and it enabled me to get a passport. So I made my way into that beautiful country. I toured all the spots I had planned to see, but what was originally a short visit extended for two years, during which I got to know the beautiful landscapes of the Orinoco and the Caroní. I met some Curacas in those regions. They walked about unnoticed, with no mental noise and with no fears.

I discovered that they came to the city of Upata or to Callao to sell gold. Then they would buy salt and other foodstuffs and travel back deep into the jungle. Once a Curaca invited me to visit his community. When he saw me working with their bees, he told me I was a man who could speak to the bees. I noticed they were located next to a river which had a large amount of gold in its bed. They treated it with respect. They only extracted from it what they needed for their subsistence.

For their buyers, the amount the indios sold them wasn't enough. They wanted it all. Although the Curaca was very smart, the mestizos stalked him until they finally found the location of the gold river bed. A gold rush ensued in the whole region and that was the end of that indio community.

When the Venezuelan government found out about this, they militarized the river, and from that moment, "the General" became the owner of the ranches and the dredges. All this led to the death of the gold river bed.

I spent a few months getting to know that country. By the time I was ready to leave, I realized my visa had expired. I had to go through many customs offices and checkpoints where I wasn't very welcome, due to my nationality. On a previous occasion, when I was on the beach, in Isla Margarita, a police officer stopped me and asked for identification. I instantly showed him the papers he requested. In spite of having all my documents in order, he took me to the police station and locked me up in a cell, where I had to spend a whole day. I kept asking the police officer for an explanation, but he just kept silent What got me out and enabled me to continue my journey was keeping calm, and paying a small bribe.

Now I had a challenge, to leave Venezuela without any document to prove my stay, which would cause a strong sanction. Therefore, I had two options.

The first option was going by land, which meant passing through several states, each of which would have two or more checkpoints or customs offices. The second option was taking a plane, which was also difficult. I decided to risk the second option.

The point of departure for the flight was Bolívar airport. The national guard would be checking documents and luggage there. They would inspect each passenger, one by one. I sent my weight down to my feet, forgot my head, and went through, showing only my flight ticket to the young lady at the check-in counter. She stamped my ticket and indicated my gate number without asking to see my passport. I joined the line where two guards were searching for hidden weapons before the passengers were allowed to move on to the boarding area. When I arrived in Caracas, just as in all *large cities, I had the impression the guards were even more scared than I was. Everyone was highly stressed and in a great hurry. I picked up my suitcase, walked slowly, let go of my fear, and moved forward firmly, without looking at anyone. I walked past the guards and without standing in line, went straight to the place where documents and luggage were being inspected. I handed over to the clerk the ticket I had purchased to go as far as the border, and he stamped it. I felt a pair of eyes on the back of my head. It was one of the guards. I thought of my boots and directed my gaze towards them. I directed all my thoughts downwards and boarded the flight to San Antonio de Táchira. From there, I crossed the border in a taxi, thus confirming that leaving behind the noise of one's mind really worked well.*

Nowadays, perhaps this anecdote may seem meaningless, because many things have changed. King Oil has left big scars in that country, and they will last for several decades. I hope, in a not too distant future, some political leader with the soul of a *Curaca* will come to its rescue. Someone who truly loves the land, because there is where the greatest wealth lies.

I left part of my fear of the past in the stream. I'm saying "part" because the next day the therapy continued with a new orchid.

"This one is better, Timoté. Drink and surrender yourself to it."

It was another day, and I still hadn't recovered from the previous experience. Clearly, Cuatiendioy had established a rhythm and didn't want to interrupt it. I felt that everything I had experienced and reenacted in my mind was so present that I didn't believe it was advisable to continue with another orchid. Or maybe I was afraid of what I might find. But I couldn't disobey Cuatiendioy, who always knew what he was doing.

I drank the water, and sat down to observe the surroundings. I felt scared again. I didn't know what I was afraid of, but I was uneasy. Cuatiendioy had said, "Anyone who moves about very much is scared. Watch the rabbit. It's an easy prey for any predator.

A little bird is in constant movement, unlike a cat, who lies down and sleeps peacefully. The *civilized man* is afraid of losing everything; he's never relaxed. The *civilized man* has no peace. He moves about a lot. He's always seeking for everything outside himself."

For my part, I was aware that I was afraid, but I didn't understand why, which was all the more reason for being annoyed by that. So I tried to relax, went back to memories of my birth, and perceived my parents' fear at that time. Their lot had been to live through a war, and I had been born right in the middle of it. So I was the fruit of their love, but also of their fear. In that wonderful country, two individuals created a stupid war, with all the ensuing bloodshed, and they split the country in two. They created two opposing sides and assigned a color to each: blue and red. My father and his brothers hid in a cave which was in the middle of a huge rock that looked like a meteorite. It was so tall that it could be seen at a great distance. I saw *Don* Emilio's eyes again, as he watched me. Those blue eyes, penetrating, sparkling and calm, said to me, "Don't be afraid. Everything is calm out there." *Don* Emilio gave me permission to be calm, at least during my childhood. I remember him walking up from the village to our ranch, with the patience of a snail. He never complained about anything. There was always a fresh smile on his lips.

Cuatiendioy observed me while I threaded together the events from my birth and from my childhood. The fear subsided as I gradually became conscious of it. I told Cuatiendioy about my experience with *Don* Emilio and he said, "Every event in your life happens for a reason. Every encounter brings its own messages. I think it's enough for now of working with the orchids."

VIII

Allies In The Jungle

"It's a beautiful day for collecting honey," said Cuatiendioy. "But today it's the turn of the ones that sting -the Africanized. We need to be very careful with them. Permission is different. We must try not to mistreat any of them. Any mistake could be fatal. These bees aren't from here. They've caused trouble ever since they arrived. Or actually, since the *civilized man* brought them from Africa. The other ones from Italy weren't from here either, but the jungle had already accepted them. Now the *civilized man* doesn't know how to take the trove away from them. They call them "Africanized." They don't realize that their spirit is more rebellious, just as some *indio* communities, our brothers whose spirit does not accept the spirit of the *civilized man*.

"Well, now the *civilized man* is trying to exterminate the Africanized bees, just as he wants to exterminate some of our communities to take possession of their land. But these bees won't let them. They aim to dominate the jungle, and they are achieving their aim. The *indio* has already figured out their quirks and managed to make friends with them. Today we're going to seek them out and take away some of their trove. Of course we need to be very careful, watch the movements around their entrance, ask for permission from the sentries, and reassure them that we only want to take a portion and that there will be no aggression.

"We'll take a lighted cigar with us and apply some mellow puffs of smoke so they'll get the message. The smoke makes them alert. It'll be a struggle with no resistance. You'll see, Timoté."

He whistled several times into the wind, and the bird showed up. He whistled again and the bird alighted instantly.

"Today, he'll show us a swarm of bees or a beehive. Don't think he'll do it for free. He's expecting his reward. Just wait a bit and you'll see what his payment is. This will be a happy day for him. He knows exactly where the beehives are. He'll lead us to the nearest one."

Cuatiendioy whistled again, but differently this time, and the bird began to imitate his sounds. It went into the thicket, flying low, making a big fuss. It flew almost as low as the height of our heads. Then it alighted on a rock.

Cuatiendioy had prepared a kind of cigar with some tobacco leaves. He took out the two flint stones from his bag. Then he made a compact bundle with some dry twigs and leaves. Rubbing the stones together, he lit the bundle and then the tobacco. Finally he said, "Wait here. I'll go see what I can do and how much we'll be able to work with them."

After inspecting the beehive from up close, he said, "Not these, they're too weak. They won't have a good trove. Besides, it's hard to extract here. They've barely started, and the hive won't yield even a single drop."

He whistled to the bird again. It continued its flight while we followed it through the thicket. It alighted on a withered tree and whistled to Cuatiendioy.

"These are easier. I'll go check how strong they are."

He went near them and came back smiling, "Before we start, I want to give you some instructions. We need to remember that we're intruders today and we've come to steal part of their trove. We need to do it without causing offense, respectfully and carefully just as with everything in nature. It's all in what kind of start we make. We need to do it right. Imagine, Timoté, that this is your house and someone comes in to take something that you have and he needs, but you don't want to give it to him. You know there's going to be trouble. So you measure how much you are willing to give him, and you give it to him provided he asks for it delicately, without violence. That's what it's like in the jungle. First we ask for permission from the sentries by showing them the smoke."

We went up to the entrance. Cuatiendioy inhaled from the cigar several times and let out the smoke around the entrance, after drawing circles with his hands over the agitated colony, slowly and harmoniously.

"First rule: never stand in front of the entrance. It's a lack of respect for the bees that are arriving from the outside, loaded with pollen. You're also blocking the way for bees that are flying out of the hive. They will see you as a troublesome intruder and as they are not carrying any load, they can sting you. When they do so, they'll release their alarm liquid, and all the others will come at you prepared for war. May that never happen. If it does happen, cover yourself up in smoke, to counteract their alarm smell. Watch how I'm asking the sentries for permission by showing them the smoke."

And letting out several puffs of smoke, he gradually drew nearer to them, always taking care not to block the entrance.

"For them, it's a danger warning. They recognize the smoke from forest fires. When there is smoke, they load up with honey and wait for the danger to pass. You mustn't make their eyes sore. This can happen because they don't have eyelids. The smoke has to be cold and not the kind that can cause soreness. See how they're calming down? This is the moment to act. If they're not keeping still, like they are now, you'd better not stick your hand inside the hive. You wouldn't live to tell the story."

I watched him closely. He moved as carefully as if he were defusing a time-bomb.

"We won't be able to see the queen here. It would cause a lot of chaos if we tried to. Everything you do to nature that disturbs *her, she* will respond to with an equivalent reaction, either immediately or in her good time. As you can see, the colony is calm. If your actions to extract the honey are aggressive, then that will be the nature of the impact on our bodies, because we are the creatures who are disturbing the harmony of the jungle. To avoid causing disorder, it's best to make a covenant. Have you thought of one already?"

I was fascinated by the marvelous world of insects. At the same time, being surrounded by them made me feel scared.

"Don't move too much. Here's the tobacco. Smoke a bit. Make slow movements as you smoke, so they won't see you as an aggressor."

So I smoked a little while Cuatiendioy introduced his hand into the hollow of the withered tree trunk. First, he cleared the entrance, gently pushing aside leaves, twigs and barks that were joined together by a dark-colored sticky substance (propolis). He carefully made cuts in three honeycombs, while indicating that I should gently puff some smoke in. The honeycombs contained honey and some offspring in their lower portions. He piled them up on some green leaves. Then he covered them carefully, which gave the pile the appearance of a kind of *tamale*. Some drops of honey had fallen around the entrance and immediately some bees came out to clean them up.

"I'll cover up the entrance for them again in a little while," he said.

He carefully replaced the cover he had cut off with his knife. He puffed some more smoke in, to clear the entrance without harming any bee. He used some clay to covered up every hole. Then, he explained, "This is to save them from having any conflicts with the ants. Make sure there are no drops of honey left, Timoté."

By that time, the bird was impatient. It flew in circles around the hive. It whistled and Cuatiendioy whistled back with a special kind of whistling one they could understand. Cuatiendioy picked up the honeycombs carefully, traced a circle with his hand, contemplated the colony once more, and we set out towards the *temascal*.

As we walked back, he said, "Humans don't understand the consciousness of insects. They expect them to think as humans do. They want to have everything and they respect nothing. That's how they've always behaved. They arrive, they mistreat the bees and they kill hundreds or even thousands of them when they want to take their trove. But that won't happen with these bees. *They* don't yield so easily. They demand more respect. They will teach the *white men*. You'll see how they defeat them, Timoté."

I never imagined that years later, I would witness the arrival of Africanized bees in Mexico, after having won their battle in South America, and after having defeated the *civilized man's* resistance, just as Cuatiendioy had said.

México was preparing with all kinds of traps and strategies. I could see the money that was spent trying to destroy them and remembered Cuatiendioy's wisdom. At the same time, I asked myself how many other things we were doing wrong, with or without consciousness, in our efforts to see everything under the microscope of rationality.

The African bees —*Apis melliferaadansonni*— passed, having taught humans to have a bit of respect for bees. Before them, there were few apiculturists. The majority were all "honey merchants." But they were forced to become apiculturists and respect the insects' demands. So at least, they started to apply more rational methods of exploitation, by using adquate equipment and taking better care of the bees. Of course we are still very far from true harmony with nature, but "some day it may be," as Cuatiendioy used to say.

We got back to the *temascal*. The bird was still impatiently flying in circles right above our heads.

"What does the bird want, Cuatiendioy?"

"His reward."

"What's that?"

"You'll see."

He unwrapped the honeycombs, cut off the sections where the offspring or larvae were, and placed them on a rock. The bird alighted and immediately started eating them.

"That's why the bird leads you to the beehive, Timoté. This is his reward, his treat. We only go harvesting for honey three times a year. The rest of the time, he's my company, my ally. He doesn't care about time. He doesn't measure it. In the meantime he eats fruit and seeds He knows there will come a day when I give him the signal that it's his time. Patience is rewarded. He'll eat now. Then he'll go back to waiting again for another four months. He knows where all the hives are and he loves eating the larvae, but he can't get to them. That's why he's my ally. He does his part and I do mine. Find yourself an ally."

"And, how can I do that?"

"With your feeling. They can perceive what you're thinking."

Without having fully understood his comments, I walked away for a while, searching for silence. It turned out that my silence lasted several days. Time didn't matter. It was all about being, abiding. Before that moment, I had had very little understanding of the peacefulness that one experiences in silence.

We spent many days without uttering a single word. Words became less and less necessary as time went by. I obeyed every instruction Cuatiendioy gave me. Sometimes he communicated through subtle gestures. Sometimes I could read his thoughts. Sometimes he'd look into my eyes and I would obey instantly. With his mind, he would get me to stand up, sit down, move away or draw near.

One day, he told me, "One thought at a time. Focus all your energy on one thought, until you achieve your aim."

When I heard that, I was instantly reminded of my schooldays. Very often I would come to class without having done my homework. On such occasions I would look the teacher in the eye, and silently repeat, "Not today, Sir." And sure enough, they would call on any other student, but never on me. And whenever I *had* prepared adequately for a lesson, I would also look the teacher in the eye but what I'd silently repeat was, "Call on me first, Sir". And they often did. I wasn't a good student during my first years in high school. I didn't like the city, so I was constantly doing things that might force my father to bring me back to the farm. I didn't like my teachers' methods either. They manipulated my knowledge and my learning, by not teaching me how to feel, and much less, how to see. Sadly, they had never been taught this either. So I tried to survive this short period of my life making as little effort as possible.

"A healer must be healthy himself," Cuatiendioy remarked. "His mind must be empty when he sees his patients. He mustn't have any thoughts whatsoever, and he must let the patient's body show him his or her pain. So if you silently ask, "how are you going to heal youself?" they will tell you. They know what will cure them. But the noise in their mind doesn't let them see it.

"When energy is blocked, it becomes toxic and causes illness, just like water when it doesn't flow. A healer has to move the energy; he has to move the stagnant water. He has to touch in order to heal. Touch the soul. When they won't let you touch their soul, that's when you need to use the flowers, the orchids. You can also use stones; they have healing properties. You need to be very concious of the place you are taking them and need to ask permission before you do it, and you also need to know where to place them on the human body. You have to look into the patient's eye. Always look at their eyes, never at their pockets. Doctors determine the gravity of the illness depending on the amount of money in the patient's pockets.

"Some doctors prescribe so many things that the patients are cured by the impact when they see the prescription. Sometimes the wallet hurts more than the pain. Some day you'll see, Timoté."

"Why should I? I'm not a healer. I'm going to be an agricultural engineer. I like the countryside and I'm going to farm my land."

"Poor Timoté, how confused you are. I think we've been in this spot long enough. We'll be leaving soon. The rains are coming again and with them, the cold southern winds. We're going to a community nearby. It's about three days' journey from here.

IX

The Flight Of The Condor

"You mean we'll be seeing other people?"

"That's right. And possibly we'll be meeting people who have never seen a *civilized man* before. Don't forget to become one with them. They're *indios* who may seem different to you, but they are less sick than the *white men* are. We won't be seeing *white men* yet. It wouldn't be good for you. *White men* would contaminate the work you're doing.

"Why is that, when I'm *white* myself?"

"You're *white* and you're *indio*. You've learned many secrets of the *indios*. The ones you've been allowed to learn. Maybe they'll listen to you now."

I remembered that a few days before setting out from the North of the country, in the most humid region of the continent, during one of our walks in the Chocoana jungle, on the border with Panama, while we were looking for medicinal plants, we heard some strange noises coming from the thicket. Cuatiendioy was walking slowly and in silence. I followed behind, carrying a pile with several plants. Suddenly, we saw a group of half naked *indios* coming out of the thicket. They were picking seeds from some trees. The men carried spears and the women carried the seeds in their baskets. Their hair was white. I felt that was very strange because I had never heard of white-haired *indios*. But there they were. As soon as they saw us, they pulled out some rattles and started shaking them near their ears to avoid hearing us. Cuatendioy told me to hide behind the foliage of a tree nearby. He followed them slowly and returned soon after. He remained silent. I supposed they had accepted him.

He told me we were going to move away from that part of the jungle. He explained, "They don't like you. They don't want you here. They won't listen to you and they don't want to see you."

"I don't like them either. I wasn't looking for them. I was only curious about their hair, I replied."

I was a bit worried now. I feared that I might not be accepted either at the new place we were going to with Cuatiendioy. I was eager to meet other people and I was happy that Cuatiendioy was inviting me to meet *indios* of the Amazon, but I was also worried they might reject me. I assumed we were going to visit his own people, so just to confirm I asked, "Are we visiting your people?"

"Of course not! All *indios* are my people, but my own community and my family are far away from here. And Grand Chief Tandioy hasn't accepted you yet. We're going to a another community which is nearby."

I felt I had been confined in the depths of the jungle for a long time by then and I really looked forward to talking with someone else. I wanted to find out what was going on out there in the civilized world. I also looked forward to seeing someone other than Cuatiendioy. I remained wide awake all night. I was eager to set out on our journey, and was looking forward to new events.

The next morning we dismantled the *temascal* and gathered our few belongings: the two precious flintstones, several *guajes* filled with orchid waters, roots, and many bunches of dessicated medicinal plants tied up with *liana* fibers. With the care of a sacred relic, we also carried a *guaje* filled with honey. Cuatiendioy presented me with a gift of three rare roots, which had a fragrance that was pleasantly distinct. He explained they were called *waira*, *coco* and *chundú*, and then said, "Carry these three friends always with you. They are your protectors." He put them inside a small green bag that was tattered and poorly sewn and instructed me to hang it around my neck.

I remember very well the search for chundú—a marvelous root of a fern that was harvested during nightime only once a year: on June 24th. This was the only time I knew the exact date, which was also the only time I participated in the search of magical roots, the ones I used to hang around my neck. Everything that seemed impossible for my mind was completely natural for Cuatiendoy: communicating with plants and animals of the jungle was as natural for him as it was natural for me to communicate with my schoolmates. With the utmost easiness, he closed his eyes, entered into a deep silence for a few minutes and under the darkest night illumined only by stars and our own eyes, he asked me to follow him which was difficult due to the darkness, but for him it was like walking in plain daylight, until we arrived at a spot where the beautiful root would yield us her treasure.

We greeted the root with respect and sat down across from her. Cuatiendoy asked me to keep my eyes open with the gaze down toward the roots, which I imagined was due to the lack of visibility. We stayed like that for quite some time until suddenly we heard an almost imperceptible sound as something began to move underneath the soil. Cuatiendoy took my hand, and instantly our eyes, hearts, and breathing became one until we both dissapeared into one conscience, and empty void. Cuatiendoy explain to me that one can also use stones; they have healing properties. You need to be very concious of the place you are taking them and need to ask permission before you do it, and you also need to know where to place them on the human body.

The fern left exposed her tiny roots that sprouted from her center, a birthing process that was as natural as that of any other living creature.

Cuatiendoy dropped my hand and with intense care extracted several roots that were offered to us by the beautiful fern, and after we thanked her, we carefully placed the treasure in the pouch and went back to the temascal.

This was Chundu, the root that connected us to the Earth, when I took the root with my hand and placed it on my heart, the unique fragrance calmed my mind and everything became clear and lucid. I then took this precious gift and hung it around my neck and with a deep bow of appreciation, we left the temascal to enter again into the jungle and Cuatiendoy began to whistle to summon our bird.

Cuatiendioy walked at a continously increasing speed and I could barely keep up with him. I kept thinking about the forthcoming experience, wondering what the people would be like, what customs they would have, what their meals would be. My mind rambled just as it did when I was a child and my father would promise to take me to the village nearby. This was on Sundays. I would go over our preparations and imagine the village full of people who would stop to greet my father and pat my head affectionately. Suddenly, Cuatiendioy turned to me and said, "We won't make much progress this way, Timoté. Let go of the noise in your mind and become one with my stride. Gaze downwards and shift all your weight downwards."

I started keeping my eyes on Cuatiendioy's feet and imitated his movements. I merged into his rhythm. The jungle became greener and more beautiful once more. We seemed to be floating on a magic carpet. The insects became larger again. My senses were sharpened. There was a harmonious sound in everything.

The bird flew right ahead of us, indicating the way. Then the song of the night came, with its magical sounds of crickets, frogs, nocturnal birds and rodents, all singing in harmony the most beautiful melody. We kept up our rhythm and walked perfectly well in the dark. Sometimes a portion of sky would be visible through an opening in the foliage above, and some stars would timidly lean out to be seen. In every tree, in every branch, there were inhabitants of the jungle flashing the brightness of their eyes at us. I could feel the life of the jungle, observing us, following our footsteps respectfully, without interrupting our rhythm. Suddenly I realized our bird was no longer flying above us. It had alighted on a branch. It was part of those eyes that guided us through the night.

"No more!" said Cuatiendioy. "This is where we stop. Pass me a *guaje*."

I handed him one of the three I was carrying. I was immediately overcome by such exhaustion that I wanted to pass out. I just dropped my backpack on the ground, fell on top of it as if someone had pushed me down, and instantly fell fast asleep.

The next morning I still felt tired. I woke up with the sun on my forehead. It was cold. The land we had been walking on sloped upwards. Cuatiendioy pointed out that we were near a river source. "We're on high ground here, but go bathe," he instructed. "The colder the water is, the better. So you can start getting used to the cold."

My body ached so much all over that I thought I wouldn't be capable of diving into the river. But following his instructions, I plunged into the water abruptly. When I came out, Cuatiendioy was waiting for me with a smile on his face. He said, "I did the same thing you did. I've already bathed. Touch my body. It's warm. Come over and make these movements with me."

I couldn't listen to what he was saying. I just wanted to run, warm up my body, cover it up, find some heat.

"Come near me and watch. Copy these movements I'm making, since you can't remain one with the jungle. If you did, you'd be able to see what a monkey does when it's cold, or a tiger, a wildcat, an eagle, or any other animal. It's in their nature to know how to extract energy from the earth to protect themselves from the weather. Watch my feet and my arms. Separate your feet, stretch your arms out sideways like an eagle. Imitate the eagle. Move your arms slowly and rhythmically, as if you were flying. Crouch down slowly, with your feet firmly planted on the ground, and dig your toenails into the soil, like claws. Move back upwards to a standing position again, without losing your rhythm, feeling that the energy flows upwards through your feet and flows down through your hands. The heat that is generated right below your navel has to flow all over your body. It flows down again into the earth, comes in again through your feet, flows up your spine like a flame lighting your body until it covers you up completely. Try to do it. Today, you'll be a condor. Fly with me. Don't think. Just repeat these movements with me and forget about everything else."

Cuatiendioy started making his movements and I imitated him. Standing upright, he stretched out his arms sideways, with the palms of his hands facing upwards and began crouching down until his body was in full crouching position, with the palms of his hands facing downwards. Then he started moving back up to a standing position again, with the palms of his hands turned upwards and his trunk perfectly upright. I was very cold and wanted faster movements, like running, or walking or starting out on our journey down the slope and away from that cold area. But I was forced to adapt to Cuatiendioy. He was the one who set the rhythm, so I tried to follow him. I watched him closely and began to discover a different Cuatiendioy. He had become one with his movements, imitating a condor in full flight, moving upwards and downwards, moving his arms like two beautiful wings. There was sweat running down his arms. Now he kept turning his head to one side and to the other. His eyes were wide open, gazing fixedly, without blinking. I felt I was actually seeing a condor in full flight.

Judging by the weather, it seemed we were somewhere in the Andes Mountains. The clouds were lower than the crags and from these awesome heights, we could see only the white peaks of the frozen summits. There was a cold wind that blew through the tree canopies and whistled an eerie tune of oblivion, of distance and of loneliness—like a cry of sorrow and of grief from the gods of the jungle.

Everything was white down below, like a velvet cloak covering the rest of the world under its mystery. I had no choice but to copy Cuatiendioy's movements. The alternative was to end up frozen like the landscape below. I began to follow him, to imitate him. I found it hard to do. My hamstrings ached. At first I found it impossible to focus my mind on my navel, as he had instructed. But when I managed to achieve a dose of concentration, I was able to accomplish it.

I started moving my outstretched arms upwards and downwards at the sides of my body, while twisting the palms of my hands alternately upwards and downwards. At one point I felt I was going to leap into that vast chasm. But without losing my rhythm, I continued imitating his movements. I clung to the soil with my toes, and stuck my nails into the earth as if they were claws. I fixed my gaze on Cuatiendioy, sweeping the spaces with my eyes, as if I were searching for something. I kept my spine perfectly upright, like an oak rod, going up and down. Instantly, I felt a pleasant warmth below my navel. The warmth started to spread until it covered my body all over and I began to sweat, just like he did. His body seemed to be made of rubber. At the same time, it looked so weightless that it seemed that the cold wind would sway it. Our heads kept turning to the left and to the right, with our eyes wide open and our gazes fixed. I lost sensation of my legs and my hamstrings. I could only feel my body from my waist upwards. And my wings carried me above and beyond the thick mist that dampened my eyelids and sent water dripping down my face.

Then the cold disappeared. My movements were slow, rhythmical and accompanied by completely abdominal breathing and my wings were outstretched over the white mist. I was in a spell, following Cuatiendioy's flight. He made me feel I was really a condor. I could no longer feel my feet. I felt I was floating in the air, like a condor.

We were unequivocally two condors challenging the heights. In my fullness as a condor, I heard our companion bird above my head. The one that would appear suddenly and then instantly disappear into the thicket, like a ghost. There was only an echo of his cry, which later shifted away to a greater distance. Cuatiendioy assigned no importance to the event. But the bird came back flying lower and passed nearer to us, almost brushing our heads. Then he glided away towards the chasm. We were simply two condors, in leisurely flight, never losing our rhythm, free condors in full flight, floating over the Andes. I don't know how long we were like that, but I actually forgot my exhaustion of the previous day. My body was ready to continue the journey on foot. Flying had left me a feeling of plenitude. With my imagination, I had traveled all over the Andes.

"So, now you know, Timoté, don't you? That's what flying is. To be a condor, all you need to do is to imitate the condor, to get near to it so you can try to feel what it feels; to become a condor in your mind."

That day I felt I had flown. I felt it in my body. I'm sure there wasn't a big difference between reality and my experience. On previous occasions, Cuatiendioy had encouraged me to imitate a tiger. Although I tried several times, I had never achieved an experience as vivid as this one.

"That's all for today," said Cuatiendioy. "Now tell your body that if you didn't get sick under these conditions, you will never get sick from now on. Tell that to your body and confirm it to yourself in your mind."

"All right. I'll do that."

And we began the descent.

X

Encounter With Other Communities

We had been walking for a long while and suddenly, Cuatiendioy stopped. The bird started getting restless. For Cuatiendioy, there was a clear warning of danger.

"Timoté," he said. "There are *white men* nearby. I don't like this. Look for some branches; try to hide beneath them. Don't let yourself be seen." He handed me the bag with his belongings and slid away like a tiger in the thicket. After a short while, he came back. "It's them. *White men.* They've been able to come this far. Poor jungle! Even here you are contaminated."

For Cuatiendioy, the *civilized man* in the jungle was like the plague. For me, they were simply people, and I wanted to talk with them. Cuatiendioy insisted, "It's too soon. They'll contaminate you and I'm not done with you yet. I'll go over to see them because they're sick. They're guerrilla fighters who lost their way, most probably while fleeing from the army after a clash. Some of them are wounded. You'd better set up a *temascal* here and wait until I get back." He selected several plants from the ones we had collected on our way and set out to where the guerrilla fighters were. I obeyed his instructions: I set up the *temascal* and sat down to wait for him.

Cuatiendioy was away for two days. It was the time required for the fever to go down for those who had malaria, and also the time he needed for treating the fighters who were wounded, in addition to helping them all find a way out. When he got back, he said, "This isn't good. These conflicts between *white men* affect us more than they affect them. They fight and kill each other only for power. We don't care about their quarrels and their wars but they put us right in the middle of them. The guerrillas want our support and the government kills anyone who supports them. All we want is to be left in peace in our own lands. We've never asked for more than that."

I had been in places where there were armed clashes all the time. I preferred not to hear about them. But I couldn't suppress the need to express my protest. So I took out my pencil and wrote,

With so much lead inside men's chests,
the whole country melts down.
The air melts away little by little.
A silence of smoke rises up
that suffocates, suffocates.
Motionless, the mountain range
weeps for the tree that was beheaded.
The voice of the fields cannot be heard:
it is felt on all four sides.
The rifle is another wind
that withers the crops;
it blows sorrows in the skies;
it humiliates the dawn's birdsongs;
and on its tracks, the birds
fly away, weeping, weeping.
The rain falls upon men's chests.
Dodging the trenches,
under the leaden skies,
rains of Causes
like flags flutter in the wind.

When I had finished and put my pencil away, Cuatiendioy said, "A sheet of paper and a pencil are as deadly as a bullet in a rifle. The danger is that sometimes they can be aimed against the one who is writing. Be careful, Timoté."

That afternoon he spoke to me about his ancestors, about groups and communities they admired because of their knowledge and progress. He spoke about the Chibchas who were the best farmers; the Cunas, who were the greatest craftsmen; the Coguis, who were the philosophers of Sierra Madre; and the Guajibos, the greatest warriors.

"We were all one and the same energy, each one doing what they had to do, until the *white men* arrived. And look at us now. They never stopped killing others and killing each other. Wherever they go, they are armed to the teeth. What eyes have they got for the jungle when they only use it as a hideout and as a place for destruction? With what eyes will they understand the earth when they can't understand themselves? They bring hatred, Timoté. They are sicker in their inner selves than in their outer body. We're continuing our journey tomorrow. We're already near the community we're going to visit."

That afternoon we enjoyed some delicious tea and we roasted some bananas. The next day we set out on our journey. By then, I could easily keep up with Cuatiendioy's rhythm of walking. We made better progress. Walking at his rhythm paid off at the end of the day.

As we were getting closer to our destination, Cuatiendioy relaxed his rhythm. At one point he stopped, placed his belongings on the ground and pushing aside some branches to clear the view, pointed with his finger, "There's the community."

A few straw huts could be seen in the distance. He observed for a few seconds and said, "This isn't right. There's no smoke. Everything is silent. There are no messengers."

"What messengers? Do they also have birds?"

"No, Timoté. They have their own messengers, besides the dogs."

We walked down to the huts and found that everything was abandoned. Cuatiendioy crouched down, took a handful of dirt from the ground, and said, "They're gone."

He looked around for more tracks, and estimated the time frame by studying the footprints and the dung.

"They left around eight days ago. They surely heard the sounds of *white men* in combat."

We inspected the huts. They were completely empty. It was a lifeless place. The huts were truly works of art crafted with intertwined palm leaves. No metal had been used in their construction. This were signs that they had little or no communication with civilization. I searched in the bushes nearby for some metal pot or bucket or industrial scrap. I only found fragments of *guajes,* polished stones and sticks. This confirmed they had no contact with *white men.*

"Where could they have gone, Cuatiendioy?"

"To some place where they won't have any encounters with *white men.*"

I sat down and reflected. "How could they have abandoned their home? Where might they be?" While I considered these questions, I imagined a little *indio* child coming out of one of those beautiful huts or an *indio* woman, carrying a *guaje* on her shoulders. It was as if there were a memory that was alive in another dimension and everything spoke to me. Or maybe that energy Cuatiendioy spoke about was imprinted onto every detail where a human hand had been laid. But the space itself was also alive, it spoke of something, and the echoes of the voices sounded recent. Encompassing both sorrows and wonder, I visited all the spaces of the community, while Cuatiendioy inspected the huts one by one and introduced his hand in each of them from the outside, as if he were trying to examine something by touch. He repeated the procedure with several of the huts and finally said, "This one. We'll light our fire here."

I felt uneasy. I didn't understand yet. Cuatiendioy observed the bird perched on the tallest tree.

A flock of parakeets was squawking noisily, very near to the huts. Cuatiendioy went to find out why they were making such a fuss. I followed him through the thicket. We saw they were pecking at the few cornstalks that were left in the furrows. We cut off some cobs. I noticed the crops were not planted in tidy rows, like they did on my father's farm. Here, banana, *yuca* wild bean and *ñame* were all mingled in the same planted field. It was as if we had found a greengrocer's store. But Cuatiendioy only gathered some of the tender corn cobs. Before cutting them off, he asked for permission from the plant. That evening we had a delicious meal. The architecture of the hut was beautifully crafted with straw and reeds. Judging by its location, this one was a special dwelling. It was built right under a leafy tree, and near the stream. I slept placidly and in a slightly meditative state. Here, in spite of the solitude, there was a memory of home warmth.

I woke up feeling homesick. Everything was calm, until our companion bird made a strange squawk. Cuatiendioy swiftly stood up and said, "We've got visitors."

We quickly went over to see who, or what, was prowling about, but we saw no person or animal. Cuatiendioy kept on whistling and the bird responded, until a strange sound came from the surroundings. Near the thicket, a man suddenly appeared. He was wearing a loincloth and held a spear in his hand. He was an *indio* who recognized Cuatiendio and indicated with hand signals, that he didn't want to see me. Cuatiendioy told me to leave and wait for him in the forest until he came to fetch me. Meanwhile, the *indio* turned his back on us to avoid seeing me. I felt upset by his attitude, but I did as Cuatiendioy said and went away for a walk while they had their conversation.

After a long while, I heard Cuatiendioy calling me. While he searched for dry wood to light a fire for breakfast, he explained what had happened: The *indios* had decided to leave and settle deeper into the jungle, on the one hand because of the invasion of drug dealers who set up hideouts and *coca* processing labs in the jungle, and also because of the clashes between guerrilla fighters and the government's army.

Although these events were happening in areas that were distant from their community, the *indios* sensed their presence as being too near and therefore decided to move away. Finally, Cuatiendioy mentioned that the Chief or *Curaca* was angry about all these invasions and the felling of trees in the jungle.

For all those reasons, the fact that I was a *civilized man* created a conflict in their friendship. Cuatiendioy tried to convince the warrior that I was different and could be his friend too. Finally he told me I could come with him when he took the dry firewood to the hut, but that I should try not to look the other *indio* in the eye. I did as he told me. When we got to the hut, I acted with indifference and set about preparing the tea. They continued their conversation in a dialect that was unknown to me. Cuatiendioy disagreed with their decision to abandon their land and their homes. At one point, they both crouched down and began making marks on the ground, as if they were drawing a map. Then the topic of conversation veered to me. This was easy to infer, since they pointed at me several times.

Cuatiendioy stood up while the other *indio* remained seated on his haunches.

"Timoté, we're going to backtrack. I need to see my friend, Guaco. He's the chief of this community. We're one and a half days' journey away from them. Although, as you know, this warrior does not agree with letting you see their new location, I'm trying to persuade him that at least we can travel together, and you can wait at some other spot nearby. In the meantime, we'll have tea and eat some fruit."

He filled his bowl and took some tea to the warrior, who was still sitting in the same posture. The warrior pulled out a fur pouch. From it, he took out a kind of small, meaty coconut, which has seeds that are rich in oils (*chontaduro*). He handed several seeds to Cuatiendioy and indicated, signaling with his finger, that he should offer me only one. Cuatiendioy retorted by signaling "two." After some reluctance, the warrior consented.

Cuatiendioy handed them to me while he said, "We're doing fine."

He told me to hang up the plants we had collected and which we carried with us rolled up into little balls. The procedure was to fasten each one of them to the eaves of the hut to ensure that they would dry adequately. We hung up hundreds of them, and then he said, "They'll be safe here. If anyone comes along, the last thing they'll be interested in are these. We'll hide the *guajes* in the taller branches of some leafy tree."

I asked Cuatiendioy whether it made any sense to retrace the route we had taken on our way up to here. I argued that he already knew how his friend was and that the warrior had given Cuatiendioy all the news he needed to know. So what was the point of backtracking to go to a place where I was not accepted?

"Look, Timoté, Guaco is my friend. I've always visited him here, or wherever he happened to be. Now more than ever, I must visit him. This is the time to show my friendship now that he's going through a difficult situation. When a friend is truly a friend, distance or obstacles can't prevent you from being there with him, to listen, to see and to feel. That's what true friends are."

As we set out on our journey, the warrior gave us a handful of *chontaduro* seeds. We chewed on some and walked back into the depths of the virgin jungle again.

The warrior led the way, setting a rhythm that was different from ours, which made me feel tired and aware of the distance sooner. The jungle grew progressively thicker and darker. Sometimes we seemed to be lost. In spite of my significant experience in the jungle, I had the impression we were always in the same spot, especially in moments when I felt scared. When I embraced silence, everything was different. It had a new charm about it. But now, whether because of the warrior's rhythm or because of the difficulty of the trail, I felt very uneasy. We were approaching some marshes. They were swampy, flooded, and full of mosquitoes. The warrior said we had to cross the marshes, but Cuatiendioy proposed we should spend the night in the place where we had stopped and to cross the marshes when there was daylight. The warrior agreed.

There was a cloud of mosquitoes that was starting to seriously disturb me and we hadn't brought the herbs we normally used as mosquito repellents. The warrior had no problem with mosquitoes, but noticing my discomfort, he went over to the marsh and brought back some plants that he blended and rubbed between his hands until they became a smelly dough-like mixture. He handed me the mixture and showed me how to rub my face and body with it. The mosquitoes backed off instantly. We spent the night in the cambuches I had already grown accustomed to, covered up with leaves.

Although I was not happy with the change in our route, I reflected on the meaning of friendship. *I remembered my father, who was also a friend to others. As a child, I had seen him go out on stormy nights, in uncertain conditions, to visit a friend who was ill. On other occasions, I had seen him carrying a neighbor on a makeshift stretcher, improvised with sticks and bed sheets. My father was a friend to all his workers in the coffee plantation, who were given access to over thirty varieties of fruit, bananas, beans, corn, and sugar cane, which were abundant and which he shared with all of them. He didn't sell the fruit because his business was coffee. My mother, for her part, grew vegetables, and raised chickens and pigs. She also helped in the selection process of coffee.*

There was abundance, peace and harmony, in spite of the difficulties faced by nearly all Latin American farmers when it comes to obtaining fair prices for their crops. There have always been crooks and usurers who exploit them. My father was also exploited but even so, there was peace.

Then the saviours of the world appeared, coming to inform us that the system was corrupt and had to be destroyed because it did not longer serve the people. After spreading a lot of information and subversive propaganda, they set up several camps, and the ranch became their provider of foodstuffs. The saviours claimed they were hungry, so they needed to slaughter a cow now and then to feed all of the boys. The same applied to chickens or whatever they wanted. At first they would ask for permission, then it became a habit, and finally it became a free-for-all. Some time later the defenders of the fatherland appeared, and punished my father for "collaborating with the subversives." They were hungry too and again, a cow had to be slaughtered now and then, a few chickens, or whatever they wanted. Of course, requested with all due respect, which ended up in their doing it without permission and without any respect.

I began to understand why the natives of this community were fleeing so far deep into the jungle. *My father had fled deep into the concrete jungle. He had abandoned his farm because when he ran out of cows, pigs and chickens, the saviors of the world began to demand that he hand over to the "cause" every cent he owned. This same people that preached justice destroy the heritage of my family. My father died contemplating the mountain from a house he bought in the outskirts of the city, wondering why he had been made to pay for that Cause he had never understood.*

The fighting that had seemed to be for noble causes to serve the people was now only for money, waged by criminal organizations, or simply for private gain. I remember my father on the day he died, sitting as usual, with his gaze lost in contemplation of the afternoon, handing out all his possessions, so he could leave this world as free as he had come to it. After requesting that his ashes be cast onto the sea, that there should be no weeping and that we should purchase candy and toys for his grandchildren instead of buying flowers for his funeral, he sat down on the chair where he always sat and contemplating the surroundings, said good-bye to it all. I was right beside him. I felt my father was searching for something amongst the clouds. I felt he had a long journey ahead of him and that now, in his silence, he was waiting for my approval before departing. I had been observing him and asked him, "Father, how do you feel?

"I feel that my body is old and tired, but my spirit is free and renewed. I hope I've been a friend to you as well as a father." He continued, "A

friend is always a friend, he never hides from you, even if death says it must be so. Friends never stay and never go away. Friends are. They live on as spirits, in memories and in objects. If time and distance make you forget the memories of a friend, then he wasn't a friend. He was really a ghost."

And he continued contemplating his last afternoon, while the tres pies (the striped cukoo bird) sang in the garden.

In this space, I was able to see what a friend was, and to understand the *indio's* fear of having contact with the *civilized man*. That afternoon we went some distance away from the marshes, because a cloud of mosquitoes prevented us from making any progress. We set up a *temascal*, lit a fire, and the warrior burned some aromatic herbs which repelled the mosquitoes again. That night the warrior offered us *cazabe* for dinner (a simple cake made with *yucca* flour) and we prepared our customary tea. The damp ground was uncomfortable, but my exhaustion proved more powerful and I immediately fell fast asleep.

Our awakening was rather noisy. Very early in the morning, the warrior caught a *lapa,* which is a cute little animal, similar to a guinea pig, only larger. It has brown skin with white stripes. Up to that moment, I hadn't eaten any meat. Cuatiendioy never hunted animals for meat. Actually, he wasn't at all interested in hunting. We had always made good meals with other foodstuffs and were fine with that. But he didn't mind that the warrior had killed the animal which he was now preparing for us to eat.

Cuatiendioy watched him silently as he sharpened the sticks on which he was going to insert the meat. At one point, he turned to me and said, "Timoté, you'd better eat this little animal, even if you'd rather not. Make sure you accept everything the *indios* offer you. For them it would be an insult, a humiliation, if you don't drink or eat whatever they give you. We'll be arriving at their community today. I'll be giving you several instructions which I hope you will follow, for your own good. Another thing: don't look at their women! They go about half-naked here, and the *indio* does not like the *civilized man* to look at them. If they offer you one, you'll have to chase after her in the thicket. You'll know what to do in that case. But the important thing is that you must not look at them."

The warrior took a piece of roasted meat, held it up to the sky, and started to dance and sing while at the same time uttering beautiful words which I didn't understand, but I supposed he was giving thanks to his god. We also danced, stomping on the ground, imitating the warrior. After the brief ceremony ended and with due respect we ate our meal and went off to cross the marshes.

We came to a shelter built with branches, where the warrior kept his small skiff. The skiff was made of trunks, fastened together with vine tendrils and there was barely enough room for him in it. Cuatiendioy told me we would build one for the two of us. The warrior helped us with the construction. We used trunks, held together with vine tendrils and *lianas,* just as he had. We added some leaves and checked the tightness of the knots to make sure it would float well.

When everything was ready, the warrior took out a sharp, strong stake. Before clenching it between his teeth, he said something to Cuatiendioy, who took out his knife and also clenched it between his teeth. We climbed onto the skiffs and floated into the marsh, using poles to push ourselves forward. I immediately saw that the water was full of crocodiles. I had never seen so many of them together in my whole life. I was starting to be overwhelmed by fear. Cuatiendioy pulled the knife out of his mouth just long enough to tell me, "Row to the rhythm of your breathing. Keep calm. You have no other tool but your calmness."

He clenched the knife between his teeth again and went on rowing as if he were enjoying himself in an amusement park. The warrior was right ahead of us. His attitude was the same as Cuatiendioy's, but he was especially alert to spotting anything that moved. For me, it was an experience of grueling anguish for many hours. The crocodiles followed us all the time. The huge trees prevented us from seeing the sunlight.

Finally we came to a stream that flowed into a river, which in turn flowed into the Amazon river. It was late, almost nightfall, when we left the river. We continued walking deep into the jungle, almost completely covered by dry leaves, creating mysterious labyrinths in the jungle, that only the warriors were able to decipher as they became one with their surroundings. Only by following the warrior's stride I was able to came out victorious from this natural labyrinth. But I was already feeling uneasy.

Why did they have to choose such a remote place? Later, I understood. This was exactly what they wanted: that no one should be able to find them. A place with no neighbors, no *white men*. I was sure they had achieved their aim. So much so, that I began to have doubts about whether the warrior knew where he was going. But I could see that Cuatiendioy was very calm and that reassured me. Just when I was thinking about how I'd forgotten the reason that had brought me to places like these, I noticed that Cuatiendioy was smiling at me, with his gold tooth.

"So," he said. "It would have been better to do military service. Right, Timoté?"

I felt annoyed, but I just answered, "I hope this *indio* isn't lost."

"From what?" he replied. I said no more. I just continued walking behind him.

"Timoté," he said. "It seems that you haven't learned much. You've missed the best part of this journey. Don't you think it's time you started applying what you've learned? It's been a long time since you last *listened*. You haven't *seen* again. You no longer *feel*. All your suffering is your own fault. Don't blame the warrior or me for your own inner noise. At any moment now, all your anger may be transformed into sickness, into symptoms. If it happens, I want you to be aware of this. I don't want you to bring your noises to the *indios*, because if you do, they won't accept you. Become one with everything. Become one with the unpleasant conditions. Unpleasantness is an illusion of the mind. You think these people are suffering because you measure them with your own understanding of what suffering means to you."

"I'm worn out," I said.

"Of course you are! You've been walking as only fools do. You never became one with the trail, much less with my footsteps. Your noise won't let you. You express it in your footsteps."

In that moment, I realized my footsteps were the only ones that could be heard. The two men seemed to be almost floating above the ground. They moved noiselessly even when they treaded on leaves, while I kept stumbling over them all the time. At one point, I heard our bird singing and I realized I'd completely forgotten about him. Sometimes he would fly high, moving far away from us, and then he would come back to check on our progress from up close.

I was just starting to become one with the journey and began to enjoy it by synchronizing my steps with my breathing and enjoying the company of my friends who never showed any sign of uneasiness.

. when the bird made the same strange noise he had already made on a previous occasion. Cuatiendioy was about to tell the warrior to make a stop, but the man was already holding his bow and arrow and rubbing a liquid onto the arrowhead, which I supposed must be some snake poison.

"What's the matter?" I asked Cuatiendioy.

"It's the jaguar. He's already spotted us and he's hungry. There's another law here, another space. But it's not our law. Maybe the warrior will have to fight him. Don't worry. And don't let your enemy come out. You know what I mean: your fear. For a time there, I believed you *had* learned something, but now it seems you haven't. If you keep calm, you'll be able to walk without the jaguar seeing you. You must understand this is a fight between the two of them. It isn't our fight. The jaguar has walked many times right beside you and he has never harmed you. I'm going to repeat this for you: It's *their* fight. No one is going to hunt a jaguar who knows he's being hunted. It's more likely that he will end up hunting you. Look at his tracks. They're imprinted in the mud, and the water hole isn't full yet. He's nearer to us than I expected. We need to retrace our steps."

The warrior saw the fresh footprints and took a step back. He raised his bow and arrow and aimed at the treetops, while he walked backwards with the stealth of a cat. We formed a circle to protect each other's backs, and at that very moment we heard some strange noises coming in our direction. The warrior made a sound putting his hands over his mouth. A short while after, we heard a noise echoing his. I had a feeling of strangeness about this exchange. But then he made a similar noise and the response came back instantly. I realized he was communicating with someone. The sounds had been the *indios* who were hunting down the jaguar. The sounds grew louder until finally, the warrior went out to meet them.

Cuatiendioy fell into a profound silence. He seemed oblivious to the danger of being devoured by the jaguar.

He said again, "This is their war. It's like the war amongst the *white men*. It's their war, not mine. I don't accept it. That's why it doesn't affect me."

Then the warrior approached us and spoke to Cuatiendioy. I didn't grasp what they were talking about. With so much noise, the jaguar was surely far away from here. At that point I realized we were surounded by *indios* who were walking along with us, on each side of the trail, but without letting themselves be seen. Judging by the amount of movement, it was clear there were many of them.

We came to a beautiful spot, full of luxuriant trees. The warrior told us to make a stop there. Cuatiendioy said, "This is where the community is, Timoté. I'll go over to greet Guaco, and if he accepts, I'll come back for you. If he doesn't, then we'll be on our way tomorrow. Lend me something that belongs to you!"

"Like what?"

"Something fom your backpack. That sock will do."

"Why only one? Take both of them."

"Poor Timoté. Don't think Guaco is going to try on your stuff. It's just to check your energy."

He rolled it up, put it into his bag, and went off with the warrior.

"What if the jaguar comes?"

"It's not your war. Don't worry," he said, as he walked away, out of my sight.

It was late and the concert of the macaws was beginning. The monkeys were noisier than usual, and so were the frogs and birds of all sorts and species. In the meantime I sat on my battered backpack, waiting impatiently to find out whether or not I was accepted by the *Curaca,* or Chief. Just when it seemed I wouldn't be able to keep my eyes open any longer, Cuatiendioy showed up with two warriors who led me to the community. He warned me once more not to look at the women. When we got there, I was more stimulated by the smell of firewood burning than by any prospect of seeing their women. Here I was the weird one, the different one. My attire was in worse condition than Cuatiendioy's, but I was still a *civilized man.* To them, I was a curse that had come to that secluded spot of theirs, someone who could betray them and reveal their whereabouts some day.

Cuatiendioy had spoken well of me. I had to live up to the expectations he had raised, so although I felt all their gazes on my shoulders, I just walked behind Cuatiendioy and didn't look at anyone. I also knew they were laughing at me, maybe because of my appearance, which I wasn't really aware of because throughout those many months in the jungle, I had never had a mirror.

We came before the Chief, who invited me to drink out of his *totuma* a fermented beverage called *chichi.* I drank and felt I was drinking fire. I passed it to Cuatiendioy, who had a sip and returned it to Guaco. Guaco had a sip himself, and passed the drink back to me again. In this manner, we emptied I don't know how many *totumas,* until I finally passed out.

I woke up late the next day. I had slept on a hammock made of palm fiber. I don't know how I got there. Through the mesh, I could see that the women sat in a circle, separate from the men, who wore only loincloths and were standing around Guaco and his visitor. Some of the women wore a kind of skirt made out of a rough fabric, which seemed to be weaved from coconut palm leaves. They wore nothing over their breasts. Other women wore loincloths. The children were stark naked.

The community members went about their chores rhythmically and in a quality of silence that was almost meditative. They had celebrated Cuatiendioy's arrival. He was a messenger between two worlds. He walked about freely and unnoticed amongst the *white men,* like a sage from the jungle. And here he was now, flashing his gold tooth as he smiled, while these young women, with their lovely breasts exposed to the breeze, made cute flirtatious gestures at him and smiled alluringly. Cuatiendioy did not show the slightest interest in the girls. As for me, I spied them through the fiber mesh of the hammock, while pretending to be asleep. Some of them had tanned faces, black eyes, long straight hair, almost down to the ground, and virginal breasts. Their feet were wide. Some of them were weaving baskets with plant fibres while others decorated the baskets, painting them with *achotes* and other dyes, which they kept in *totumas* (dessicated pumpkin gourds).

The children were grinding seeds. They used stones for this and then extracted the colors. Some of the women had breasts that were so saggy and overstretched that they nearly came down to their knees, as if they had nursed the whole tribe. These women were weaving hammocks while they nursed their children. I wanted to take a good look at all of them, to avoid the temptation of looking in their direction when I got up from the hammock.

From my comfortable vantage point, I could observe the whole community in action. I could tell they had only recently settled here, because the hammock I had slept in was in a hut which was still under construction. There were gaps in the roof, and the intertwined reeds that would be used in the thatching were spread on the ground. This hut was built to house a whole family. I estimated that it had room for about forty people, so it was surely a family composed of several other families. There had been ten huts in the community they had abandoned. The huts had been laid out in a semi-circle. They were starting anew here. First, they would have to build Guaco's hut.

The strings of *moriche* palm leaves were also ready, as well as an amount of reeds, earth, sand, straw and dry branches, piled up in front of the hut.

Two women were using sticks to stir something in a large earthenware cooking pot which was placed on a campfire. Sometimes it looked as if they were slowly cooking their own overstretched breasts. This was because their breasts would swing back and forth to the rhythm of the stirring. One was almost expecting them to put the breasts into the pot.

Everyone was busy with some activity, except Guaco and me. We were both still under the effects of the *chicha*.

Cuatiendioy walked about, measuring distances with his footsteps, driving stakes into the ground. At one point, he would remain motionless for a long while, with his eyes closed, just as he did whenever he was setting up a *temascal*. Once he told me, "Never do anything without feeling. Especially regarding the place where you're going to live. Spaces are alive, and you need to feel whether that life is the one you are seeking for."

And here now, he kept measuring distances, and feeling spaces. I got up and asked him, "Cuatiendioy, would you like me to help you in any way?"

Everyone around us instantly burst out laughing. I thought they were all laughing at my offer to help Cuatiendioy. But it wasn't that. What they found funny was the way I spoke, my dialect, which sounded very strange to them. In addition to my way of speaking, the clothes I wore were also very strange for them. As soon as I got up, several inquisitive children started following me, and speaking to me in their strange dialect. This was very embarrassing because I needed to urinate. I went some distance into the thicket, but I couldn't shake them off. So I did what I had to do right before their eyes. They didn't mind this at all. For them, it was absolutely natural. Then I realized the young women were also watching me. They had hidden behind the bushes and observed me from there.

The incident didn't affect me at all. I'd had a good rest and now I was contemplating the surroundings. It was a beautiful spot, on the higher ground of this area. There was a delightful stream running through it. All sorts of wildlife could be seen on the white sand of the streambed. I wondered how they had managed to find such a beautiful space amidst the harshness of the surrounding jungle.

I went back with Cuatiendioy who was still busy with his task of measuring spaces and feeling places. Only now he had his arms outstretched sideways, forming the shape of a cross. His eyes were closed and he was moving very slowly, rotating almost imperceptibly. He would stop for a few moments to observe the trees, or other points of reference, recording the distances in his brain.

I reflected that if *white men* applied that construction method, they would still be building Rome.

A gorgeous young woman began to shake a rattle, calling everyone to their meal. They all formed a circle around two huge earthenware cooking pots. There was a delicious smell coming from the steaming hot food. Everyone held a bowl in their hand, which was a gourd made from wild pumpkin, cut in half and dessicated, with designs engraved on them. Guaco brought his own bowl and ours, which seemed brand new and had beautiful engravings on them that were cut with a sharp instrument showing a hummingbird sucking a flower, and one eye looking through a colorful leaf made of vegetables and a mix of crushed insects. According to Cuatiendoy, red and black were more important.

My ecstatic eyes under this subtle beauty were asking who in this community was the artist that was able to create such a wonderful art in these simple artifacts. It aroused my curiosity to find out what was their true essence, when suddenly I got closer to Cuatiendoy to watch his gourd, which was engraved with a monkey carrying her baby on her back, another baby in her hand, and a symbol of the sun.

According to Cuatiendoy, each family was responsible for designing their own gourd or *totuma*; some of the gourds narrated the family history. The ones we used were only used during special ceremonies or occasions.

In that moment, I wished I could speak their dialect, so I could communicate with them and learn about the meaning of the artwork portrayed on those beautiful bowls.

Guaco and Cuatiendioy sat right in front of the pots. Then the elderly members of the community made another circle around them. Next came the warriors, the children, and finally, the women, who formed a wonderful motherly circle that felt as if it were protecting all the rest of us. I took my bowl and while I inspected it closely, I sat down in the children's circle. The men laughed at me because my place wasn't there, but the children had already accepted me.

A short while after, the gorgeous young woman handed out a grey, sticky creamy porridge made from banana flour. Following Guaco's singing, we held it up to the sky, giving thanks to the earth for life. The song was a kind of litany that ended with the words ¡yay yay! (that was the only part I sang).

I focused on observing the bowl, to avoid remembering what I had seen in the preparation of the porridge. I had to struggle a bit, but I managed to find it had a homey taste. After all, this was going to be my family, 'who knew for how long' -with Cuatiendioy, you never knew when the next departure would be. He would nearly always tell you on the spur of the moment, or one day in advance, at most).

Finally, we all ate until we were fully satisfied. Each one went down to the stream and washed their own bowl, rubbing it over with sand. I washed mine, taking great care not to damage its decorations or harm its color.

The day went by quickly. I tried not to interfere with their activities, but I noticed that their supplies of foodstuffs were quite low, and I asked Cuatiendioy what was the source of the community's subsistence. To which he replied, "The same source as you've subsisted on all this time! And hunting! Become one with them too. Otherwise, you'll leave this place without having learned anything at all."

I had come to think Cuatiendioy and I were experiencing an adventure, but now I realized that the life of the *indio* was a permanent adventure. I needed to become one with them, just as Cuatiendioy had warned me. I was already slipping into the routine of watching. I needed to empty my mind more, in order to be able to feel what was going on.

"And what should I do, Cuatiendioy, in order to become one with them?"

"Whatever you feel!"

I took a good look at all of them, but I couldn't think of anything. I felt I was a stranger here, but at the same time I wanted to make myself useful. As I walked over to the hut I saw the children, who were bringing dry firewood. I joined them in their search and collection of wood for the campfire. We piled up the firewood in the middle of the open space of the community, as Guaco had instructed. It was quite late, almost nightfall. I was expecting the usual cloud of mosquitoes, but suprisingly, there were none. The charm of this place was always enhanced by a magical concert of sounds and chants from the birds singing farewell to the day. The branches from the centenary trees were rocking back and forth to the rhythm of silence and the wind and releasing their withered leaves with the sway of the breeze.

Once the music of the wind ceased, the time came for the evening concert. The community gathered in a circle around a bonfire that illuminated everything around and by that time all the younger women looked so beautiful. Those black eyes, so dark that they resembled the night reflecting the innocence of the constellations, and their spontaneous smiles sounded like the water bathing their beautiful and virgin bodies. Their long, beautiful, and thick hair was braided with vegetable fibers of beautiful colors dyed by artists with the intent of attracting other men in the tribe.

Only a loincloth, and the colorful headband—two seductive garments—were adorning these beautiful adolescent woman.

The meal was *casabe* (a preparation based on *yucca* fruit), *chontaduro* (the fruit of a variety of palm tree), and *petaco* (a soup made with wild beans). The same ritual, the same chanting, although the magic of the night was unique and unrepeatable.

Everyone was preparing for a magical evening, with flutes, rattles and drums. The elderly women, painted up with *achotes* as if they were models in a fashion show, walked about displaying their enchanting flirtations. Everything was done in silence, showing respect for the bonfire. Guaco guided the community in a guided ritual characterized by a special magic accompanied by the sounds of the flute, bells, and drums.

Two men appeared, each one playing a rustic flute. One of them was making a soft sound, the other a sharp sound. Another man was playing a drum made of some animal hide shown as a trophy; he was hitting the drum with a closed fist and the sound reverberated through the jungle.

After the drum was silenced, another sound from the other corner of the community with rattles was heard without being able to see who was playing the instruments, followed by other sounds coming from the other extreme of the community using flutes, drums, and rattles.

All the players stopped playing music when a loud sound from a drum was heard. At that moment all players from the four corners walked towards the center of a bonfire that was maintained by an old man who was stoking the fire in sync with the rhythm of the music. Once everybody was around the bonfire, a loud sound from a drum signaled the group to play for the last time that created a beautiful melody around the fire. After a few minutes, we all entered into a deep silence.

Finally each one sat at their place, Guaco and Cuatiendioy right next to the fire, the elderly men in the next circle, then the warriors, and in the last circle, the women, both young and elderly. The children didn't participate in this event. They watched from the construction site of Guaco's hut.

Cuatiendioy said, "Timoté, sit here and help me with this."

He handed me a rattle and showed me how to follow the rhythm. The night was becoming magical, the fire was growing stronger, and we were all fascinated contemplating it. Two men brought a large earthenware jug which contained a beverage called *yagé* or *ayahuasca*. While the men were carrying it, the women turned their backs on them to avoid seeing it (because if they did, this would deprive it of its magic). The men covered the jug with a blanket made of a rough fabric, and the ritual began. Guaco stood up chanting and beating with a thin stick on a hollow log. Next there were rattles, flutes, and a drum, which was played by Cuatiendioy this time. The women moved to the left and the men moved to the right. At the same time, they all sang a kind of litany that ended with the words "*ay ayay*." Those were the only words I repeated.

Cuatiendioy, Guaco and I remained seated while the dancing continued around the enormous bonfire, which seemed to grow increasingly stronger in resonance with the chanting.

After a long while, Guaco struck against something to produce a loud, sharp noise and we all fell silent. The men received the *yagé* beverage in their *totumas* while the women looked the other way, to avoid draining the power of the *yagé*. According to Cuatiendioy, no woman could see or touch the plant, and much less could they drink the beverage, because it was a ceremony for warriors. The men drank the *yagé* and continued with their dancing. Guaco invited Cuatiendioy to drink from his *totuma*. Cuatiendioy drank and did not allow me to drink the beverage.

"This is not your path. I don't want you to be lost," he told me.

The chanting became more excited, and there was a change in the tone. When one of the warriors cried out loudly, all the others stopped. They left the circle, took up their bows and arrows and their spears, and in a kind of trance, followed him into the thicket. The warriors had sensed the hunt.

The women went on dancing. The music again changed its tone. We waited expectantly. It was all a ritual asking *Alyagé*- the spirit of the Ayahuasca plant, to help them make contact with the prey.

Some time later cries of joy were heard and the warriors showed up with two wild boars. They offered them to the fire. They sprayed them with their beverages, while giving thanks. The women began to prepare them, while each one searched for a place to end the night.

Early the next morning, the rhythm of activities became more intense. It was the appointed day for the completion of Guaco's hut. All the materials were laid out an waiting to be used: the clay, the straw, the water and the sand.

Cuatiendioy gave instructions on how to fasten the reeds with flattened vine reeds and *moriche* palm fibers.

Three walls were built because the front part of the hut had to remain wall-less so that Guaco could command a view of his whole community. The work was completed swiftly, before enjoying a delicious wild boar broth, which was served as usual with everyone sitting in their respective circles, each according to their hierarchies.

Once the meal was over, everyone went back to their tasks. Some earth was sprinkled over a bit; straw and sand were added to it, while water was slowly poured over the materials in order to make the mixture. When everything was ready, we began the earth dance.

In a circle, everyone had their arms around the shoulders of the persons next to them. They formed a human chain. With their feet in the mixture, they all jumped up and down, to the chanting of *"jujujujay, jujujujay."* When a pause was made to add some more straw, I joined the dance. I put my arms around the shoulders of the men I had at each side and felt their heavy arms on my shoulders. I could feel my feet anchored on the ground but as the chanting progressed, I felt everyone's strength as one and the same strength. We were all straw, water, sand, and clay. It was the most beautiful dance I had ever experienced in my whole life. I could feel my feet stomping on the clay, caressing the depths of the earth, and the echoes of our chants cruising across the universe, carrying the *indio's* litanies and his chants to the uttermost corners of the earth. This dance, on its own, had the power to move the universe. Or perhaps, the universe simply danced to the chanting of the *indio.*

The mixture was ready. The dancing ceased. *Guajes* became containers for transporting the mixture. Hands became sophisticated tools for flattening and binding. While some transported material, others affixed it onto the reeds, leaving their handprints on this work of architecture, as noble and wholesome as the *indio's* impeccable existence.

Cuatiendioy would check the uniformity of the walls and the finer details of construction, using a rod which he applied in sweeping movements over the surfaces. It was a beautiful and intense day. Guaco's hut was ready. But it wasn't only Guaco's hut. It was our hut. It had the sweat and the energy that had come from every one of us. The men went off to the river stark naked. They washed the clay off their bodies with leaves and sand, a type of "soap" as natural as the *indio* himself. The young women searched for a place upriver and came back refreshed and beautiful, with their virginal beauty enhanced by the green carpeting of the jungle.

In this state of deep contemplation, time went by more swiftly than usual. The rituals at mealtimes had a significance of union with the family for me, rather than of worship. Union with the family when working, and also when eating wild boar roasted on the fire and seasoned by the smoke, with its scent mingled and softened by the cool fragrance of women, recently bathed and wearing the perfumes made with fresh flower essences.

I felt that just contemplating the scene was more pleasant for me than sitting down to devour the boar. But my state of bliss was interrupted by a pair of hands stretched out to give me a *totuma*. I lifted my gaze and for an instant, I saw the bright and loving black eyes of a beautiful young woman who was inviting me to join the family circle.

Everyone slowly gathered for the well-earned banquet, so fresh and luminous, so beautiful and innocent, forming a circle as they gradually arrived. Some women had applied the pulverized petals of exotic flowers on their faces. I realized that I could easily do without the wild boar, or the other sacred foodstuffs for the body. But I couldn't bear to miss the family gathering, its rituals and chanting, that priceless and healing nourishment for my soul.

The circle was ready. We were all seated on the ground, around the wild boar, waiting for a signal from Guaco. In his role of *Curaca*, he was respected like a father who listened and provided guidance and advice to his community, without any need of written laws. His face was a philosophy book of examples. In his luminous and penetrating eyes you could see the transparence of justice.

There was a new celebration today. Guaco's hut was ready. Slowly, he walked over to his newly-built dwelling and sat down in front of it. Keeping his gaze on it all the time, he clasped his hands together, and bowed a few times. Then he got up slowly, placed his clenched fists over his heart and began to dance to the tune of a new, guttural chanting, which was taken up by the whole community and resonated throughout the luxuriant jungle.

I joined in the dancing. Instantly, I felt my body vibrating. I couldn't control my jaw, which kept moving of its own accord. I let myself be carried away and became one with the dance, and with the *indio's* guttural chanting. Under the effects of the chanting and the dancing, I vanished from the circle. I thought I was no longer in it because I could no longer feel my feet, and I could see myself floating above the circle. I was certain I hadn't taken any substance, nor had I eaten or drunk anything except some water after my task in the contruction.

When the dance was over, I felt Cuatiendioy's hands leading me to the place where they were all waiting for me to sit down so the sharing out of the wild boar could begin. An elderly woman began carving it up and and two young women handed out the portions to each member of the community, who waited in their places to be served in the customary manner.

We dined accompanied by the usual evening "concert," while Guaco addressed everyone in their dialect. It seemed to be instructions regarding the building priorities and the future layout of the other dwellings. He would point to different families and then point to the spot where their hut would be built. Architecture seemed to have been heavily influenced by Cuatiendioy, because the huts in the community they had abandoned were built only with straw and reeds.

While I was listening to Guaco, my attention was captured by a teenage girl who had a bracelet on one of her wrists. It was made with shiny colored seeds. I looked for Cuatiendioy and asked him, "Why is that child wearing a colorful bracelet, Cuatiendioy?"

"That girl is ready for marriage. Now a man must become a warrior in order to deserve her. After a ceremony, he will chase her through the jungle and court her. You've already seen that married women have a stripe painted on their feet that is not easily rubbed out. But we won't be witnessing the wedding of this lovely girl. We're leaving in two days' time. Tomorrow we'll collect honey for our journey and for the community. It's time to rest now."

XI

The Departure

That was exactly what I did. I fell asleep while contemplating the fire, as usual.

Very early in the morning, Cuatiendioy spoke to me, "Get the *guajes* and cover yourself up as much as possible. It's very damp and we don't know how these bees will react."

While I gathered the *guajes,* Cuatiendioy whistled to the wind, calling his ally. When I heard the bird's reply, I realized how much I'd forgotten about him recently. He flew down from the tree, displaying his elegant profile, cutting his flight short and almost brushing against our heads, eager to point out the location of the wild beehives. We followed him for several kilometers into the jungle until we found the colony, amidst the roots of a luxuriant tree. This time we extracted serveral honeycombs and an amount of offsprings for our ally. We returned to the community and started perparations for our departure, which was the next day.

It was past midday. Everything was quiet. The men were building the second hut. Cuatiendioy was talking with Guaco about the details of the design, which he was outlining with poles and stakes. Suddenly, a falcon started flying in circles above the community, while it uttered a strange, harsh cry. A warrior saw him and ran to get his spear and his bow and arrow, while shouting out in warning to the others.

The whole community was alarmed. A warning signal was whirling over our heads. The ally of the community was alerting us.

Cuatiendioy whistled to his own ally, who replied instantly from a leafy tree, where his meal of larvae lay. He whistled again and the bird flew up high, circling above the community. That call hadn't been to search for bees; it was for him to find out what the threat was. Instantly the bird uttered a cry I had never before heard it make. Cuatiendioy dropped to the ground, face downward and stretched out both arms sideways. Still with his ear to the ground, he cried out, "*Tambochas!* The *Tambochas!*"

All the members of the community went into a state of alarm. Scrambling to pick up the children and the few foodstuffs we could carry with us, we all ran to the stream. I really didn't grasp the magnitude of the problem but I followed Cuatiendioy, who was laboring with the men to clear away any branches from the stream, while everyone jumped into the water, right in the middle of the watercourse. We all held hands, forming a human chain again, this time to avoid being carried off by the current.

There was an instant of mysterious suspense. Then the jungle broke out in a deafening uproar. All the living creatures of the jungle ran past in terrified flight. There were none that dared challenge the *Tambochas*. Every living creature was running for its life. Hares, country mice, wild boars, deer, lizards, snakes, every living creature had joined the stampede.

In a few seconds, the whole space resonated with a pervading din, and a dark brown carpet covered the jungle for kilometers on end. The huge ants advanced, obliterating all forms of life in their path. There were millions of them inspecting every nook and cranny. Nothing escaped their lethal jaws. It was a terrifying hunting spree. It seemed that this enormous advancing mass would go on forever. It was getting late and we were beginning to feel the cold. Suddenly everything started to calm down. The *Tambochas* went on their way, and the jungle fell silent. That night, no crickets were heard, nor birds and I doubt there was a single nest that hadn't been thoroughly inspected.

Shortly before dark, all movements ceased. The stragglers among the ants didn't seem to be so aggressive. We climbed out of the stream and headed for the firepit hoping for some warmth. While some of us tried to get a fire started, one of the women pointed to the stake above the firepit where a large chunk of roasted boar had been hung for smoking. All that was left of it were the bones. The rest had been eaten up by the *Tambochas*. If it hadn't been for that wisdom and vision of the *indios*, the whole community could have disappeared in a matter of minutes. Now came the worst consquence. They had no food. How long would it be until the next hunt?

The bonfire was started, and it soon warmed us. We all drank some tea prepared by Guaco. It was so acid I found it hard to drink.

We were all exhausted and went straight to our hammocks and mats. I lay down in my hammock and reflected on the danger I had experienced recently.

I didn't sleep that night. In everything that moved out there, I thought I could see the huge ants moving. It felt like an endless night to me.

Very early the next morning, when the sun was just rising, Guaco took us to the bonfire, which was almost out. There were several warriors with us, and three women. He led us into a circle, while they danced, bowing towards the four cardinal points. He used ashes to trace some lines on our foreheads, on the palms of our hands and on our feet, as a charm for protection and good luck. One of the women used some feathers to make sweeping movements all over us. I felt just like when I was a child and my parents gave me their blessing as I was leaving home to go to school in the city.

Once the farewell ceremony was over, Cuatiendioy whistled and as usual, our bird responded by taking flight and following us. We set out escorted by two warriors who knew the water courses, marshes and swamps, some of which were infested with crocodiles and lizards.

As the jungle swallowed us up, we left behind the community, which was caressed by the breeze, cheerful with the singing of birds, and protected by the magic of the *indio*, still untouched by the *civilized man,* preserved as a seedbed that will remain when this destuctive madness is over.

Far off in the distance, when occasional gaps in the foliage allowed it, we could see the smoke rising up, in praise of the God of the *indio.*

The warriors led us past the swamps and headed back to the community. We began preparations to spend the night, before the arrival of the clouds of mosquitoes. There in our old and improvised *temascal,* I lay down with a kind of nostalgia, feeling I was leaving my family behind. We slept through the night and set out early the next morning, without uttering a single word. We made our way deep into the jungle, both of us walking at the same rhythm, and soon came to the old abandoned community.

I had rarely seen Cuatiendioy deeply wrapped up in his thoughts. This time was one of them. We had a connection from the soul by now, and words felt redundant. But not to Cuatiendioy, who broke the silence.

"Everything passes, Timoté. This adventure will pass, just as life does. One day, you'll remember all of this as a story. It's all in how one lives each moment. Joys and sorrows, good and bad, time and space, here and there; they are all the same thing. Everything is the same thing. Everything is mind and illusion. And illusion will pass, just like life. We'll soon be out of this. I hope you've found some clues. At least, I hope you've healed your past. It's about becoming one with everything until you feel you are nothing, and touching in the stillness, the furthest limits of silence. Whatever comes next, you'll have to discover it for yourself and confront it."

We were both seated on a rock, contemplating the abandoned community. He touched my backbone again and asked, "What do you see now, Timoté?"

"There's a strange silence. I can't hear the Cenzontles and the Troupial birds singing, I feel a deep sadness knowing I will be leaving the jungle soon. Nothing is as it was. Everything is expectant. I'm thirsty. The river claims its crystal clear waters from me. The plants no longer speak to me. I'm still seeking for the meaning of my existence. I'm becoming a plant. The river runs through me..."

"Fine, Timoté, we'll continue with this some other time. I'll let you know when!"

I felt the branches swaying in the distance. The bird's song was fading away. I opened my eyes to look at the surroundings. I was alone. With no fear. And very calm. The concrete jungle was calling me.

GLOSSARY

achotes: achote is a small seed which gives a bright yellow color to foods

african / africanized bees [Apis melífera adansonii / Apis melliferaadansonni] : african bee introduce to Brazil in 1956

aguardiente : sugarcane spirits

alma mater : University

alyagé : the spirit of the Ayahuasca plant

angelita bee Tetragonisca angustula : bee from the Apidae family which produces honey of high medicinal and nutritional value

boldo tea : Medicinal plant that is traditionally used by the indigenous tribes

cambuche : makeshift bed made of wide leaves

capybara or agouti : Dasyprocta rodent that is easy to hunt and preffered by the natives of the jungle

carambolo juice :a tropical fruit

casabe : a preparation based on yucca fruit

cazabe : a simple cake made with yucca flour

ceiba tree : Giant tree that can reach up to 230 feet, very lush which branches can extend up to 66 feet

chichi / chicha : a fermented beverage

chontaduro : the fruit of a variety of palm tree

chontaduro : a kind of small, meaty coconut, which has seeds that are rich in oils

chontaduro : palm fruit

chundú : a marvelous root of a fern that was harvested during nightime only once a year - on June 24th

coca : a native plant that is a complex combination of minerals and essentials oils. One of its byproducts is cocaine

cundú roots : a plant to which Cuatiendioy's people attribute magical and healing powers

curaca : someone in a position of authority and responsibility within his community

curacas / caracas : wise men of the jungle with knowledge of the healing properties of plants

guacamaya birds : native bird of South America, it lives in the tropical forests of beautiful and colorful plumages, it feeds on insect fruits and hard seeds like nuts that tend to break easily with its hard beak guaje : a kind of sun dried gourd

gualanday tea : tea from a tree native to South America with a beautiful purple bloom whose healing benefits are used for throat problems, helps the skin and relieves bone pain

guarumo tree : Yarumo tree of the Intertropical zone of height between 5 and 100 meters high with silver leaves that shine on full moon nights causing a beautiful night landscape

higuerilla bush : It has many medicinal properties. Its leaves, seeds and fruits are used, it helps the growth of eyelashes, it helps the skin in eczema and dermatitis

hueja huejahionahuejahuejaiona : indigenous song or lament

indio : native from the Amazon jungle

ixtle : fiber bag

jimerita / jimerita bee : bee from the Amazon jungle

jorongo : blanket

lapa : a small rodent, similar to a guinea pig

liana : plant organisms or plants that have no beginning or end. They look like ropes that become very difficult to develop skeins, widely used by monkeys and other animals to climb trees

mapaná snake : Poisonous snake from the tropical forest

matarratón : gliricidia sepium: often simply referred to as its genus name Gliricidia, is a medium size leguminous tree belonging to the family Fabaceae meliponineo : stingless bee: Stingless bees, sometimes called stingless honey bees or simply meliponines, are a large group of bees – about 550 described species:, comprising the tribe Meliponini

mestizos : mestizo is a term used for racial classification to refer to a person of mixed European and Indigenous American ancestry. In certain countries in Latin America may also refer to people who are culturally European regardless of ancestry

moriche palm : mauritia flexuosa, known as the moriche palm, ité palm, ita, buriti, muriti, miriti, canangucho, or aguaje, is a palm tree. It grows in and near swamps and other wet areas in tropical South America. Mauritia flexuosa, a tree, can reach up to 35 m in height

ñame : a type of sweet potatoe. The Ñame is grown in tropical and highly humid regions as a major cultivar. Africa, Asia, and the Caribbean are the major home of ñame

petaco : a soup made with wild beans

tamale : a tamale, in Spanish tamal, is a traditional Mesoamerican dish made of masa, a dough made from nixtamalized corn, which is steamed in a corn husk or banana leaf

tambochas : highly poisonous red ant from the Amazon jungle

tecolote : owl

temascal : temascal and temazcal are all forms of the Nahuatl word temazcalli which refers to a type of sweat lodge used by indigenous Mesoamericans tití monkeys : Callicebus is a genus of monkeys known as titis. Historically, titis were monogeneric, comprising only the genus Callicebus

totuma : a dessicated pumpkin gourd

tres piés / tres pies : three feet / striped cuckoo

waira coco : a rare root

yagé : ayahuasca

yuca : wild bean

yuko : a bitter root / juicy fruit

Printed in the United States
by Baker & Taylor Publisher Services